CAMBRIDGE INTRODUCTION TO THE HISTORY OF ART

The Art of Greece and Rome

Other titles in the series

The Art of Greece and Rome

SUSAN WOODFORD

CAMBRIDGE UNIVERSITY PRESS
Cambridge
London   New York   New Rochelle
Melbourne   Sydney

Published by the Press Syndicate of the University of Cambridge
The Pitt Building, Trumpington Street, Cambridge CB2 1RP
32 East 57th Street, New York, NY 10022, USA
296 Beaconsfield Parade, Middle Park, Melbourne 3206, Australia

First published 1982

Printed in Great Britain by Balding + Mansell, London & Wisbech

Library of Congress catalogue card number: 81–10091

British Library cataloguing in publication data

Woodford, Susan

The art of Greece and Rome – (Cambridge
introduction to the history of art)
1. Art, Greek 2. Art, Roman
I. Title
709′.38   N5630

ISBN 0 521 23222 8 hard covers
ISBN 0 521 29873 3 paperback

Acknowledgements
For permission to reproduce illustrations the author and publisher wish to thank the
institutions mentioned in the captions. The following are also gratefully acknowledged:
Cover, 1.11b, 1.12, 1.16, 1.17, 1.19, 1.22, 1.24, 1.25, 2.6, 2.7, 3.2 Susan Woodford; 1.3,
2.16, 2.17, 2.18, 2.19, 2.21 reproduced by courtesy of the Trustees of the British Museum;
1.4, 1.13, 2.1, 2.2, 2.4, 2.5, 9.1, 9.5, 9.12 drawn by Susan Bird, courtesy of the Trustees of
the British Museum; 1.6, 1.9, 1.10, 1.26, 1.27, 2.13, 2.14, 2.15, 2.20, 3.3, 3.15, 6.2, 7.6
Alison Frantz; 1.14, 2.3, 2.9, 2.11, 3.5, 3.6, 3.12, 3.14 Hirmer Fotoarchiv; 1.18, 1.23, 1.28,
1.29, 4.4, 4.6, 4.8, 4.9, 7.1, 7.2, 7.4, 7.5, 7.7, 7.8, 7.11, 9.8, 9.11 The Mansell Collection;
1.20 The Strange World of Mr. Mum by Phillips: copyright Hall Syndicate: courtesy of
Field Newspaper Syndicate; 2.8 Deutsches Archaeologisches Institut, Athens; 3.4 from
G. M. Richter and L. F. Hall, *Attic Red-Figured Vases* (Yale University Press 1958); 3.8,
5.1, 5.3, 5.4, 8.1, 8.5, 8.8, 8.9 Fotografie della Società Scala, Florence; 3.11 C. H. Krüger-
Moessner; 4.2 reproduced by gracious permission of Her Majesty Queen Elizabeth II; 4.3,
7.9, 7.10 Deutsches Archaeologisches Institut, Rome; 4.5 Brian Lewis; 5.2 Professor
Andronicos; 6.1a Professor J. Travlos; 6.1c from W. B. Dinsmoor, *Architecture of Ancient
Greece* (Batsford 1953); 6.3 from M. Schede, *Ruinen von Priene* (Berlin 1934); 6.5 by
Gorham P. Stevans, courtesy Agora Excavations, American School of Classical Studies,
Athens; 6.6 from H. Kähler, *Das Fortunaheiligtum von Palestrina Praeneste* (Saarbrucken
1958); 7.3 Leonard von Matt; 8.2 Editions d'Art Albert Skira; 8.3 Werner Forman
Archive; 9.2, 9.10 Fototeca Unione; 9.3 Professor Frank Brown from *Memoirs of the
American Academy in Rome*, 26 (1960); 9.4, 9.6 © Arch. Phot. Paris/SPADEM; 1.7, 1.8
(from G. M. A. Richter, *Kouroi*, 1960), 3.1 (from G. M. A. Richter, *Greek Art*) The
Phaidon Picture Archive.

Contents

Contents

Introduction

Helen, thy beauty is to me
Like those Nicean barks of yore,
That gently o'er a perfumed sea,
The weary, wayworn wanderer bore
To his own native shore.

On desperate seas long wont to roam,
Thy hyacinth hair, thy classic face,
Thy naiad airs have brought me home
To the glory that was Greece
And the grandeur that was Rome.

Ode to Helen (Edgar Allan Poe)

Poe's ode is addressed to the legendary beauty who, though married to King Menelaos of Sparta, was carried off by the Trojan prince, Paris. Menelaos thereupon summoned his allies and, having assembled a mighty army under the command of his brother Agamemnon, king of Mycenae, sailed to Troy and fought there for ten years until the city was sacked and Helen recovered. This is a famous story and one that has often inspired poets, but its connection with the glory of Greece and the grandeur of Rome may not be immediately obvious.

The myth of Helen and the Trojan war seems to have had historical roots in the period around 1200 BC. People speaking an early form of Greek were then already living in Greece and had produced a flourishing civilization that we call *Mycenaean*, naming it after the richest and most powerful of its centres. By the end of the eleventh century BC, for reasons that are still obscure, this splendid civilization lay in ruins. Populous sites had become deserted, trade had ceased, skills were lost and crafts declined. A once wealthy civilization had become poor, a literate one illiterate. Meanwhile new tribes of Greek-speaking people, the Dorians, began to move into Greece and some of the earlier ones migrated eastward to the islands of the Aegean and the west coast of Asia Minor. Hardly more than a memory survived the desolation that followed the collapse of Mycenaean civilization, but out of that memory legends were shaped, tales were told and poems again recited.

By the eighth century BC the *Iliad* and the *Odyssey* had been composed. These two Homeric epics developed the story of the Trojan war and made it into something essential for all later cultural developments. They were among the earliest manifestations of a new civilization, the *Hellenic*, which had arisen out of the ashes of the old; the people who produced this civilization, the successors of the Mycenaeans, were the ones who created the 'glory that was Greece'. Throughout their history they greatly valued the poetry of Homer; children learned his works by heart and adults used them as models of behaviour.

In the four centuries from the time of Homer to that of Alexander the Great (356–323 BC) the Greeks evolved a culture that was to be immensely influential in the western world. The conquests of Alexander carried Greek ideas to people far beyond the traditional centres in which Greeks had lived. Such geographical extension drastically modified the character of Greek civilization, and so this later phase is called *Hellenistic* rather than Hellenic. From the third to the first century BC, Hellenistic culture was admired and imitated from the western borders of India to the southern slopes of the Alps.

The 'grandeur that was Rome' came into being rather differently. Rome was founded in the eighth century BC, a small settlement on the banks of the Tiber with no memories of a glorious past. As the city grew in power, the Romans encountered more civilized peoples and began to take a greater interest in art and literature, which hitherto had been of little importance to them. At first the Romans learned from the neighbouring Etruscans (who were masters of Rome for a time and left a lasting imprint on Roman religion and attitudes), but from the third century BC they turned increasingly to the Hellenistic Greeks for instruction and inspiration. By adapting elements of Hellenistic culture and combining them with their own well-developed organizational and military skills, the Romans were able to produce a magnificent culture of their own.

By the time Rome had reached her zenith, Greece had become a mere Roman province. But even then the myth of Helen and the Trojan war continued to play a vital part in Greek culture. The Romans, when they began to appreciate Greek values, sought to attach Greek legends to their own traditions by tracing their descent from those very Trojans whom the Greeks, in their art and literature, had depicted as noble and worthy adversaries.

Centuries later Roman civilization fell into decline. The cities and sanctuaries of Greece, too, became little more than neglected ruins. Nevertheless the art of Greece and Rome, even though what has survived is only fragmentary, bears vivid testimony to the erstwhile greatness of these two civilizations. The object of this book is to recapture the feeling of the time when this art was created and to explain its lasting power to enthral men's minds and captivate their imaginations.

1   Free-standing statues

THE GREEKS

The beginnings of Greek civilization after the decline of the Mycenaeans were not very glorious. By about 1000 BC people speaking various Greek dialects were living around the Aegean sea. Principal among them were the Dorians, who lived mostly on mainland Greece, and the Ionians, who populated many of the islands and part of the west coast of Asia Minor. They gathered together in small, widely separated communities, many of which eventually developed into *poleis* ('city-states', as they are often, somewhat imprecisely, called; singular: *polis*).

The earliest communities were poor, illiterate and isolated from one another as well as from the rest of the world. Slowly they began to prosper and develop. By the middle of the eighth century BC, when the Homeric poems were being composed, craftsmen could already produce huge funerary monuments of pottery covered with precise and elegant decoration (3.3). Soon an increase in population encouraged the now overcrowded Greeks to send out colonies, east to the area around the Black Sea and west to Sicily and south Italy. The poleis eventually also began to trade more widely and so came in contact with the peoples and cultures of Egypt and the Near East. These ancient, literate and brilliant civilizations with their rich and accomplished art forms awed and astonished the Greeks. Thoroughly impressed and desperately eager to learn, many had by the middle of the seventh century BC acquired the two skills which enabled them to produce the literature and sculpture that later made them famous: they learned how to write and how to carve stone.

Each polis was fiercely independent and each developed a character of its own. Corinth, on the isthmus, was rich and luxurious, a great trading centre; Sparta became renowned for her military prowess; Argos produced a succession of outstanding bronze-casters; Athens, an Ionian polis on the predominantly

Dorian mainland, encouraged individual achievement and attracted gifted foreigners, so that eventually the finest poetry, drama and art were created there.

These independent poleis were linked by a shared language and a common religion. At the famous panhellenic (all-Greek) sanctuaries like Delphi and Olympia, the Greeks from different poleis would meet together to hold competitions in athletics, poetry, and music in honour of the gods. Most of their other encounters were acrimonious. The poleis were constantly at war with one another.

It took a great threat to unite them, even temporarily. That threat came in the early years of the fifth century BC with the Persian wars. The Persian empire had gradually absorbed the Greek poleis on the coast of Asia Minor during the course of the later sixth century BC. In 499 BC these poleis unsuccessfully rebelled against their Persian overlords and drew Greek poleis from the mainland into their rebellion. The Persians quelled the revolt and sent out a punitive mission. When this came to grief on the plains of Marathon, defeated primarily by the Athenian army in 490 BC, the Persian king resolved on a war of total conquest.

The Greeks united to face the common enemy. The Athenians, though their city was sacked, took to their ships and fought bravely in the naval battle at Salamis in 480 BC, and the Spartans distinguished themselves in the final battle on Greek soil at Plataea in 479 BC. The great Persian invasion had been defeated.

Athens had been an important and cultured polis before the Persian wars, but it was after their conclusion that she reached her height. The fifty or so years between the end of the Persian wars (479 BC) and the beginning of the Peloponnesian war (431 BC) were for her a golden age of art, literature, and political power. She continued to produce great works right up to the end of the century, but the Peloponnesian war, in which she and her empire fought against the Spartans and their allies, eventually sapped most of her strength and almost all of her creativity. Though Athens was defeated by the Spartans in 404 BC, the works she created during the fifth century BC were so extraordinary in their beauty that they have been considered classics ever since.

Archaic is the name given to the period from about the middle of the

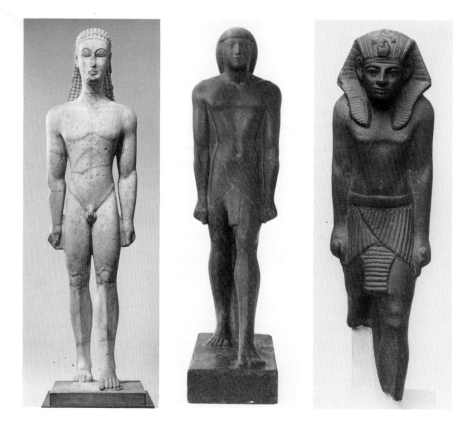

from left to right

seventh century BC (around 650), when the Greeks were first
developing techniques and ideas stimulated by contact with the
older civilizations of Egypt and the Near East, until the time of the
Persian wars in the early part of the fifth century (490–479) BC.
Classical is the name given to the period from the Persian wars till
the end of the Peloponnesian war (404 BC).

The term 'classical' is commonly used in two further senses. It
often simply denotes excellence, so that something is called 'a
classic' if it is an outstanding example of its type; or the term is used
historically, so that the Greek and Roman civilizations together are
known collectively as 'classical antiquity' in order to distinguish
them from the remoter antiquity of the civilizations of Egypt and the
Near East. In this book 'classical' is used restrictively to describe the
artistic style developed in the fifth century BC.

The archaic and classical periods were for the Greeks immensely
exciting times to live in; thinkers and practical men were constantly
discovering and inventing new things. It was also a critical time for
the development of art, as we shall see.

6

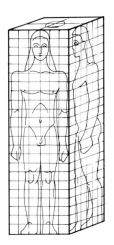

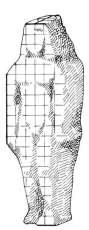

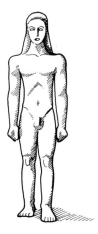

GREEKS AND EGYPTIANS: STYLE AND TECHNIQUE

Sometime after the middle of the seventh century BC, the Greeks began to carve large figures of men out of marble (1.1). They must have been impressed by statues made in other hard stones that they saw in Egypt, since the inspiration for the type of standing figure they made clearly comes from Egypt (compare 1.1 with 1.2 and 1.3). There was also something else, more important than inspiration, which came from Egypt: technique.

Carving a life-size figure out of stone is not a simple matter, and any unsystematic attempt quickly leads to disaster. The Greeks must have been aware of this. They knew that the Egyptians, many centuries earlier, had devised a method for carving stone figures. The Egyptians would draw the outlines of the figure they wanted on three (or four) faces of a stone block – front view on the front, profile on the sides. Then they would chip away inwards gradually from the front and the sides, removing more and more stone until they reached the depth that corresponded to the figure that had been drawn (1.4). The drawings had to be made according to a fixed scheme of proportions (for instance, one unit up to the ankle, six units up to the knee and so on) so that when the work was finished the front and side views would merge with one another.

The Greeks adopted the Egyptian method of working, and to a large extent also the Egyptian system of proportions. That is why early Greek statues look so much like Egyptian ones (1.1, 1.2 and 1.3).

The similarities in pose and technique are obvious; the differences in style and function are more subtle, but extremely important. The Egyptian sculptor made a rather convincingly naturalistic figure of a man; the Greek statue is more abstract. Evidently the Greeks believed that a statue of this kind should not only look like a man, but that it should also be a beautiful object in itself. They made it into a thing of beauty by imposing three elements of design on the representation of the human form: symmetry, exact repetition of shapes, and use of the same shapes on different scales.

The Greek sculptor, like his Egyptian counterpart, appreciated the natural symmetry of the human body with its pairs of eyes, ears,

1.4 Diagram showing the archaic and classical Greek method of stone carving.

7

arms, and legs, and stressed this symmetry by keeping the figure upright, facing straight forward, standing with its weight equally distributed on its two legs. He avoided any pose containing twists, turns, or bends since these would have spoiled the symmetry.

Symmetry about a vertical axis was thus easily achieved. But symmetry about a horizontal axis was quite another matter. The human form, with a single head at one end and a pair of legs at the other must have seemed unpromising material to organize in this way. Nevertheless, the Greek artist dealt with the problem by inventing his own, rather limited, horizontal axes. He imagined a horizontal axis running across the body at the level of the navel and then produced a symmetrical design on either side of it (1.5 red) – the upright 'V' of the heavy accented muscle separating the torso from the legs and the balancing inverted 'V' of the lower boundary of the thorax. He imagined another horizontal line midway between collar bones and pectoral muscles. He then balanced the shallow 'W' of the pectorals below it with the inverted shallow 'W' of the collar bones above (1.5, blue). (The symmetry is easier to perceive if you turn the book sideways.)

The sculptor repeated certain shapes exactly, in order to produce a decorative pattern. He made the line of the eyebrow follow the line of the upper lid (1.5, brown) and composed the hair of bead-like knobs, each of which is the same as its neighbours (1.5, brown). This is particularly effective from the back, where the play of light and shadow on the richly carved hair contrasts with the smooth surface of the body (1.8).

Use of the same shape on different scales is the third aesthetic device employed by the sculptor. Notice how the shallow 'W' of the pectoral muscles is echoed on a smaller scale in the shallow 'W's over the knee caps (1.5, yellow) and how the protruding 'V' of the torso–leg division is echoed in the smaller, recessed 'V's of the elbows (1.5, green).

A great deal of thought about design has obviously gone into the making of a figure that at first glance might appear rather more primitive than a contemporary Egyptian statue (1.2). The Greek sculptor has sacrificed the smooth naturalism of his Egyptian model for the sake of creating a more aesthetically satisfying work. Greek artists were always concerned with striking a balance between

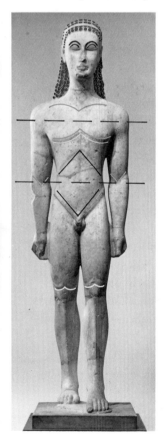

1.5 Kouros (same as 1.1).

Analysis of the sculptor's efforts at pattern making.

beautiful designs and natural appearances, though sometimes the balance was tipped towards the abstract and formal, as here, and at other times towards the convincingly real.

The Greek statue we have been looking at (1.1) was made towards the end of the seventh century BC. It is one of the earliest examples of a type made throughout the archaic period (from about 650 to 490 BC). This type of statue – a nude male figure standing facing front with the weight evenly distributed on both legs – is called a *kouros* (plural: *kouroi*) meaning 'young man'.

THE PERILS OF PROGRESS: ARCHAIC KOUROI 650–490 BC

The Greeks made kouroi to serve one of three functions. A kouros could be the representation of a god; it could serve as a beautiful object offered as a dedication to a god; or it could be a memorial of a man, sometimes placed upon his tomb. There was nothing in any of these three functions that dictated the form of the statue and nothing to prevent artists from changing that form as they saw fit. This was very different from the practice in Egypt, where statues were often carved to serve a quasi-magical function, for instance to be available as alternative homes for the 'ka' (the spirit of a man) should his mummified body accidentally be destroyed. Magic is by its nature conservative and resistant to change. That is one of the reasons why a statue made around the middle of the seventh century BC in Egypt (1.2) looks so much like a statue made over a thousand years earlier (1.3, around 1750 BC).

Change for its own sake, or 'progress', seems to us the natural order of things, but in antiquity it seemed daring, usually undesirable, and often downright dangerous. Exact repetition of a model assured the sculptor of the successful outcome of his work. Changing even one element could lead to unlooked-for and often unfortunate consequences.

The Greeks, who were adventurous and willing to take risks, found all this out for themselves.

There were, of course, technical limitations on how much they could change at any one time, since the marble still had to be cut from the block in the same way and any statue had to be designed so

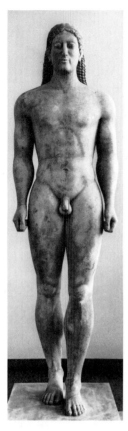

1.6 Kouros from
Anavyssos, *c.* 530 BC,
height 194 cm, National
Archaeological Museum,
Athens.

that it would not fall over or break. Within these limits, however, the
Greek sculptors started to make changes and to produce, little by
little, increasingly naturalistic kouroi.

Within a hundred years of the early kouros shown in 1.1, by about
530 BC, the kouros found at Anavyssos (1.6) had been created. This
grave marker is a splendid figure, full of vibrant life, and shows a
tremendous advance in the direction of naturalism. It is even more
natural in appearance than the Egyptian statues (1.2 and 1.3).

But the new realism of the Anavyssos kouros proved a mixed
blessing. It was achieved by modifying the proportions of the figure
and giving a more rounded treatment to the lines that had simply
been graven into the surface before. The hair however – always
difficult to render convincingly in stone – is carved not very
differently from the hair of the early kouros. Here is a good example
of the sort of problem that emerges once artists start making
changes. The stylized, decorative, bead-like hair looked appropriate
on the early kouros (1.8), because it fitted in with the whole stylized,
decorative character of the statue. Not so on the later kouros (1.7).
There the swelling, natural forms of the body clash with the
artificial, stiff, bead-like hair.

This clash of styles was not one that could have been foreseen by
the sculptor. It simply emerged when he altered some of the
traditional elements. How such unanticipated problems could take a
sculptor by surprise can be seen from a third kouros (1.9), made
around 500 BC, that is, about a generation later than figure 1.6.

The statue representing Aristodikos – it also served as a grave
marker – is still more naturalistic. It is so natural that it almost
makes the Anavyssos kouros (1.6) look like an inflated balloon by
contrast. The problem with the hair has been solved drastically:
most of it has been cut off. And yet, despite the convincing
anatomical forms – or perhaps just because of them – there seems
something wrong with the statue of Aristodikos. Why, one wonders,
does he stand so unnaturally? Why is he so stiff?

The pose is, of course, merely the consequence of having learned
how to make statues from the Egyptians; this was the pose that the
drawings on the block produced. The outlines used for this latest of
the kouroi were not basically different from those used for the
earliest (see 1.1, 1.6 and 1.9 for front views and 1.11 for side views).

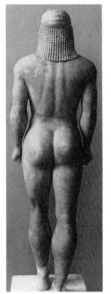 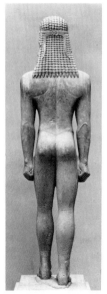 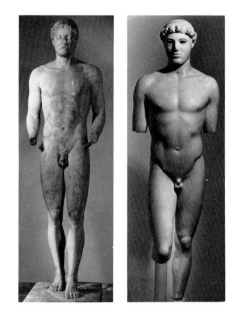

from left to right

1.7 Kouros from Anavyssos (same as 1.6), back.

1.8 Kouros (same as 1.1), back.

1.9 Kouros (Aristodikos), *c.* 500 BC, height 195 cm, National Archaeological Museum, Athens.

1.10 Kritios boy, *c.* 480 BC, height 86 cm, Acropolis Museum, Athens.

In the earlier kouroi the pose presented no problem; it is only when the figure has otherwise become so natural that we begin to question it. A gain in one direction has entailed a loss in another.

The pattern that we recognize when we look at the three kouroi – change, emergence of a problem, solution of that problem and emergence of another – is a fundamental one for the whole development of Greek art. And the failures are as important to notice as the successes if we are to appreciate the daring of the Greek artists. They could have endlessly repeated the same proven formulae, as the Egyptians did, and run no risks; but their restlessness and sense of adventure spurred them on from one problem to another. Each problem led to a solution on a higher level of complexity until finally the Greeks produced solutions that carried such conviction that they left an impression on all later western art and eventually reached the far corners of the world.

NEW MEDIUM, NEW STYLE:
BRONZE CASTING IN THE EARLY FIFTH CENTURY BC

The new problem emerging from the accomplished naturalism of the Aristodikos, the last of the kouroi (1.9), namely that the pose began to look stiff and rigid, could be solved in only one way: by changing the pose. The sculptor of a statue called the 'Kritios boy'

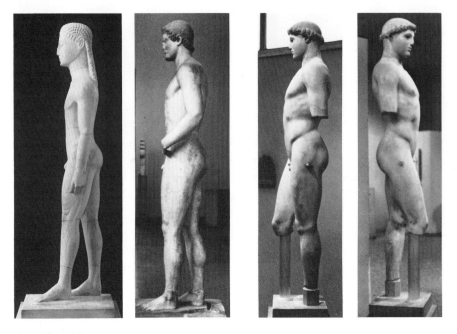

from left to right

(1.10), made shortly before the Persian sack of Athens in 480 BC, has done just that. Instead of looking straight ahead, the boy turns his head slightly. Instead of standing evenly on both legs, he has shifted his weight onto his back leg, slightly raising the hip on that side.

The physical changes are actually rather small, but the consequences are enormous. The statue has come to life.

The technical challenge was great. The outlines drawn on the block for the earliest and the latest of the kouroi (see 1.1, 1.6, 1.7, 1.8 and 1.11) were not fundamentally different, and sculptors could use the same basic scheme, modifying only the proportions and details of finish, for more than a century. The sculptor of the Kritios boy, however, had to make four radically new drawings (1.10 and 1.12).

Nobody had ever carved a statue in stone like this before.

How could the sculptor be sure that the outlines would fit together properly in such a new and complex pose? How could he know that the statue would look all right when it was finished? Experimenting with a new pose was risky in the extreme. So much could go wrong.

It would, however, have been considerably easier to experiment with a new pose if the statue were to be *cast in bronze* rather than carved out of marble. To make a bronze statue the artist would first make a model in clay (1.13, black). He could walk round the model as

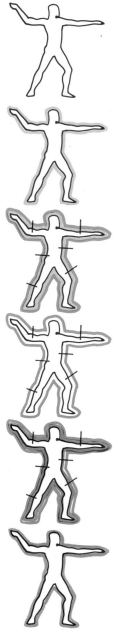

he worked and change it as he went along, adding curves and adjusting contours in a way that would be impossible for a sculptor of marble. When the model was complete, the artist would cover it with a thin, even coating of wax (1.13, yellow). The surface of the wax showed what the finished surface of the bronze statue would look like. Next, the artist surrounded the model with a mould (1.13, blue), made mostly out of clay, thick and strong enough to withstand the pressure of molten metal. It fitted neatly around the wax and was held in place by iron rods that ran through to the core of the clay model. The wax was then melted out, leaving a gap between the clay model core and the outer mould (1.13, white). Molten bronze (an alloy of copper and tin) was poured into the gap to fill the space originally occupied by the wax (1.13, orange). After the bronze had cooled and solidified, the mould was chipped away and the completed bronze figure was smoothed and finished. (The 'lost wax' method of bronze-casting is often a great deal more complicated than this, as air vents are necessary and statues are seldom cast all in one piece, but this description and the diagrams convey the essence of the process.)

Marble is a heavy material, with little tensile strength, that easily breaks under its own weight if extended unsupported over too great a span (for instance, the extended arms in figure 1.16 would be in danger of breaking off if the statue were made of marble). A sculptor has to be extremely careful that all parts of a marble statue have adequate supports. Human beings, made out of muscle and bone, can stand on one leg or even on tiptoe; stone statues cannot. Bronze, on the other hand, has great tensile strength, and statues cast in bronze can balance on very slight supports. Quite a different range of poses is therefore possible in bronze.

The Kritios boy (1.10) had been made in Athens a little before 480 BC, a critical year for the Athenians, since it was in 480 BC that the Persians sacked their city. This was one of the last episodes in the war between the Greeks and the Persians, for the next year the Greeks finally defeated their common enemy and drove the Persians out of Greece.

The Athenians then returned to their city and began to rebuild it. Most of their sculptures were beyond repair; the pieces were either used as building materials or simply but piously buried. The Kritios

1.13   Diagram showing the 'lost wax' method of bronze-casting used by archaic and classical Greek bronze-casters.

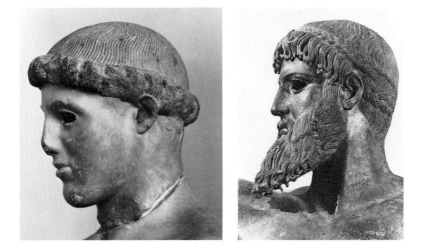

right
1.14   Kritios boy (same as 1.10), head.

far right
1.15   Zeus of Artemisium (same as 1.16), head.

boy was buried, only to be rediscovered, the head and the body separated, in the nineteenth century by archaeologists digging on the acropolis of Athens. Bronze statues had been either carried off or melted down. The stone base for one such lost bronze statue shows that it must have stood with the weight on one leg and the other leg relaxed, like the Kritios boy. Thus we know that a bronze statue in the new relaxed pose existed at about the time the Kritios boy was made.

It is easy enough to see how a statue like the Kritios boy might have been created in *bronze*, but why should a sculptor try something so new and difficult in marble? Perhaps he was struck by the liveliness of a bronze statue in the new relaxed pose. Would he not have felt disappointed when he returned to work on a kouros, even one as fine as the Aristodikos (1.9), so very life-like and yet lacking the breath of life? Every careful new detail served only to make the statue look stiffer. Nothing but a change of pose could help. He decided to risk it, to make new drawings on all four sides of his block. It would take almost a year of hard work before he would know if his attempt had succeeded. Perhaps he actually took the bronze statue as a model and a guide for his drawings. Details of the Kritios boy's head (1.14) suggest that the sculptor had been looking at a bronze statue. The hair is represented by means of shallow scratched lines. Notice especially the wisps on the neck. This treatment is characteristic of bronze technique (see 1.15), for even slight scratches show up clearly on the smooth shiny surface of a bronze. Marble does not reflect light so sharply; on the contrary it absorbs it, so that much bolder carving is required to throw a

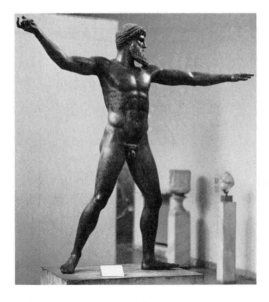

1.16 Zeus of Artemisium, second quarter of the 5th century BC, height 209 cm, National Archaeological Museum, Athens.

shadow. That is of course why archaic sculptors represented hair by means of deeply cut bead-like knobs. The use of inset eyes is also typical of bronze work (see again 1.15); eyes on marble statues were usually painted.

In the end, as we can see, this sculptor's attempt did succeed; we do not know how many others failed.

GREATER BOLDNESS, MORE PROBLEMS:
EARLY CLASSICAL STATUES

The Greeks had created, then, an entirely new kind of life-like statue. Nothing like it had ever been seen before. It made people look at statues in quite a new way, apply new standards and ask new questions like 'What is this statue doing? Is he moving or is he still?'

Such questions probably never occurred to most sculptors making kouroi during the archaic period, but for artists working in the early classical period (the second quarter of the fifth century BC), they were vital issues.

The answer for the Kritios boy was clear; he stood un-ambiguously at rest. Other sculptors sought to explore the opposite extreme: emphatic movement. That is what the sculptor of the bronze Zeus (or Poseidon) which was found in the sea off Cape Artemisium did (1.16). The god is portrayed in the midst of

15

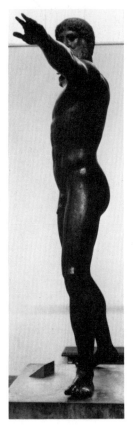

1.17   Zeus of
Artemisium (same as
1.16), side.

vigorous action, at the very moment of hurling a thunderbolt (or trident) at an unseen enemy.

This fine bronze gives us a good idea of the extremely high quality that bronze sculptors could achieve at this time. The free, open pose also illustrates why the greatest sculptors of the fifth century BC preferred working in bronze to working in marble.

Questions of character or age were not asked when archaic sculptors carved kouroi; in these respects their statues all looked much the same. By contrast, artists in the early classical period were deeply concerned about the characterization of the men or gods they represented and used every device in their power to differentiate them in terms of age and personality. One has only to compare the youthful, tender, almost shy head of the Kritios boy (1.14) with the magnificent, mature and forceful head of the Zeus of Artemisium (1.15) to appreciate this. It is not just a matter of adding a beard – archaic artists would sometimes do that to indicate an older man – but rather a profound and thoughtful distinction that is drawn between early adolescence and full maturity. (Both, of course, looked very much more convincing when they still had their coloured, inset eyes in place.)

We have seen that doing something new can easily unbalance the coherence of a work of art and that unforeseen problems are likely to emerge. This has happened with the Zeus of Artemisium. A novel sense of movement has been brilliantly captured, but at the same time two new problems have appeared, neither of which is solved.

First, though the torso should be dramatically affected by the vigorous activity of the limbs, it is as still as it would have been in a quietly standing figure like the Kritios boy. Second, though the Zeus of Artemisium is splendid from the front and the back, it is pathetically unintelligible from the sides (1.17), which was not the case with the Kritios boy (1.12) or even the kouroi (1.11).

Made at the same time as the Zeus of Artemisium in the second quarter of the fifth century BC, but very much more celebrated, was the Discus-thrower by the bronze-caster Myron. So famous was it that centuries later the Romans ordered copies to be made (1.18). Instead of having expensive bronzes cast, the Romans chose to have copies made in marble, which was much cheaper.

Such a delicately poised statue in marble could not stand up

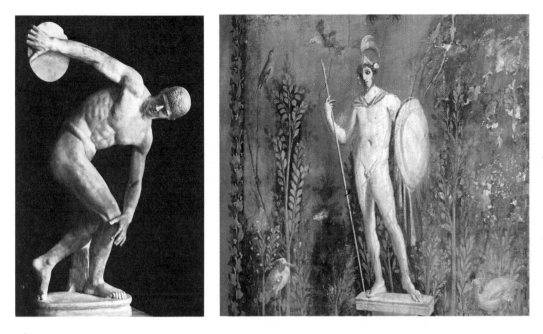

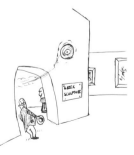

without supports and so a marble treetrunk behind the athlete was
used to help hold up the top-heavy mass of stone and to keep it from
cracking at the ankles. This might not originally have looked as
disfiguring as it does now, since all marble statues were painted
(1.19) and the supporting treetrunk would have been painted in so
discreet a colour that it would hardly be noticeable. Pupils of the
eyes were painted, too, which made the statues look lively and
responsive – the blank stares we meet in museums are the result of
the disappearance of the paint with time. Hair was also painted, lips
were tinted, clothing was decorated. We can get some impression of
an ancient marble statue with its original paint intact from a
Pompeian painting of a statue in a garden (1.19).

The original bronze Discus-thrower by Myron has disappeared
(most ancient bronzes were melted down at some time, either by
accident or on purpose) and so we are lucky to have the Roman
copies, for although they do not convey the full beauty of the
original, they give some important clues about its design.

The moment represented was chosen with genius. The Discus-
thrower is caught at the top of his back-swing, just before he
unwinds to hurl the discus. It is an instant of stillness, and yet in our
minds we are impelled to complete the action, as a twentieth-
century cartoonist suggests (1.20). But, though the pose is momen-
tary, there is nothing unstable about it.

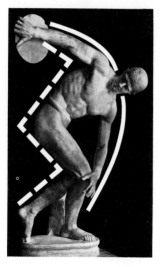

1.21 Roman copy of the Discus-thrower by Myron (same as 1.18). Analysis of design.

1.22 Roman copy of the Discus-thrower by Myron (same as 1.18), side.

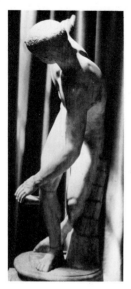

The Greeks were concerned not only to make their statues resemble men, but also to make them objects of beauty. In the archaic period, symmetry and repetition of shapes were used to produce beautiful effects. These were now out of fashion; in fact they were systematically rejected in the design of the Discus-thrower (1.21). Notice how consistently symmetry is avoided. The right side of the statue is dominated by the sweep of a continuous, almost unbroken curve (1.21, solid white), the left by a jagged zig-zag (1.21, broken white); the right side is closed, the left open, the right smooth, the left angular. The simplicity of the main forms, the great arc and the four straight lines meeting almost at right angles, brings harmony to the agitated figure. The torso is seen from the front and the legs from the side, so that the most characteristic features of each are presented simultaneously. Both representation and design are marvellously clear.

But what of the problems that emerged from the active pose of the Zeus of Artemisium? Alas, they are still there, perhaps even in aggravated form. The torso is so unresponsive to the vigorous action of the limbs that in the eighteenth century another copy of the Discus-thrower torso was taken to be part of a dying warrior and restored as such; and the side view, showing chest and legs each in their least characteristic aspects, is almost unrecognizable as a human figure (1.22).

It was up to artists of the next generation, in the *high classical* period (about 450–420 BC), to try to solve these problems.

THE CLASSIC SOLUTION:
THE SPEAR-BEARER OF POLYKLEITOS

The classic solution was formulated by Polykleitos, an Argive bronze-caster. He made a statue of a man carrying a spear and wrote a book (now lost) explaining the principles on which it was based. He was much admired for having embodied the rules of art within a work of art. That work, unfortunately, no longer exists. Once again we have to try to puzzle out from Roman copies in marble what made it so celebrated (1.23).

The Spear-bearer is shown in the midst of a step; a momentary

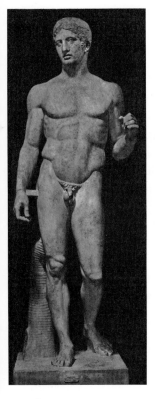

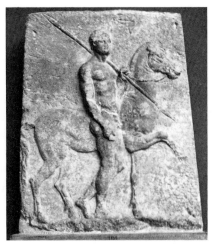

above

1.23 Roman copy of the Spear-bearer by Polykleitos, original made *c.* 440 BC, height 199 cm, Museo Nazionale, Naples.

above right

1.24 Stele found at Argos showing side view of the Spear-bearer, 4th century BC, height 61 cm, National Archaeological Museum, Athens.

pause combines stability with the sense of potential movement. The action is far less vigorous than that of Myron's Discus-thrower, but the torso is fully responsive to it. The Spear-bearer held the spear in his left hand (to our right), his left shoulder is therefore tensed and slightly raised. His left leg bears no weight and the hip drops; the torso on this side is extended. The Spear-bearer's right arm hangs relaxed, the shoulder is dropped. His right leg supports his weight, the hip is raised. The torso between hip and armpit is contracted.

The contrast of contracted torso on one side and extended torso on the other gives the body a look of dynamic equilibrium, very different from the static symmetry of the kouroi whose right and left sides are essentially mirror-images of each other. The alternation of tensed and relaxed limbs combined with the responsive torso is called *contrapposto*. It is a device that is used over and over again throughout the history of art, so effective is it in imparting a sense of vitality to figures made of stone or bronze or paint.

The turn of the Spear-bearer's head to his right gives the final touch to the statue; it describes a gentle reversed 'S' curve, one that was much appreciated in the Gothic period and used to give grace to statues of the Madonna. The turn of the head to the right adds interest to the side view, a point that was appreciated by a later sculptor making a relief (1.24) who has adopted the side view of the Spear-bearer for his own purposes.

The two side views have very different qualities, but each is harmonious and lucid in itself (1.25). The right side is tranquil, with the verticality of the straight, weight-bearing leg continued in the vertical relaxed arm. The left side, by contrast, is angular, the sharp

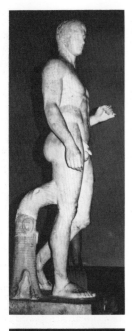

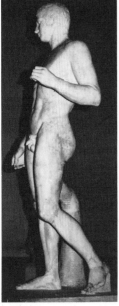

1.25 Roman copy of the Spear-bearer by Polykleitos (same as 1.23), sides.

elbow of the bent arm responding to the sharp bend of the relaxed left leg.

A great deal of art has gone into the making of a statue that looks artless. The perfect harmony that was attained in this work brought no new and unanticipated problems in its wake. This was the classic solution, one that was to be appreciated down through the ages.

STYLE AND TASTE: DRAPED FEMALE FIGURES

Though the Greeks in the archaic and classical periods liked to portray men in the nude, they preferred sculpted women to be clothed. The clothing actually worn by Greek women was loose and could be draped in a number of ways according to the wearer's choice. The artists also had considerable freedom in choosing how they would depict drapery. Drapery in all periods has provided much scope for expression, enabling artists to suggest calm serenity or agitated movement in accordance with the mood of the scene portrayed and the taste of their times.

Changes in taste often seem to have an inner rhythm of their own, almost independent of other factors. At one time simplicity is highly valued; at another, richness and elaboration are preferred. There is often a sharp reaction from one to the other. We see such changes of taste at work in modern fashions. They also influenced ancient art.

Although a statue of a clothed woman is entirely made of stone, some parts of it are supposed to look like a living person and other parts to look like inanimate but pliable fabric. A sculptor in the second quarter of the sixth century BC (575–550) was able to impart a life-like quality to the face, arms and feet of his figure (1.26) but he left the clothing as a sort of dead area with nothing more than its orderly appearance to recommend it. The many parallel vertical folds carved into the stone neither portray the soft natural fall of cloth nor suggest the presence of a living woman's body beneath it.

Artists had made great progress by the last quarter of the sixth century BC (around 525). They could now suggest the existence of a pair of swelling breasts, a slim waist, and a well-rounded thigh beneath an elaborate play of folds (1.27). Two different kinds of cloth are even distinguished: a soft, thin, crinkly undergarment

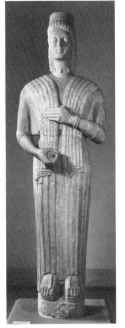

from left to right

(painted a dark colour) and a heavy woollen cloak that is draped diagonally under one breast.

By the first half of the fifth century BC (around 460), a sculptor was able to make a statue look like a woman wearing clothing. Even a Roman copy (1.28) shows how well body and drapery are integrated and how naturally they are both treated. Although little can be seen of the body, the irregular fall of the vertical folds of the skirt and the slight displacement of the material over the bosom convincingly suggest a body beneath.

The artist who created the so-called 'Venus Genetrix' (known only through Roman copies) (1.29) in the late fifth century BC has made the drapery so thin and clinging that the goddess's body is revealed almost as completely as it would be in a nude representation. One breast, in fact, *is* bare.

In less than two centuries, then, sculptors had developed techniques and formulae that enabled them to show draped female figures as living women wearing garments made of soft cloth. The progress of naturalistic representational skill is very marked.

So too are the changes in taste. In the first half of the sixth century BC drapery is austerely simple (1.26). By the end of the century it is usually shown as complicated and ornate with strong diagonal accents, a multitude of folds going in different directions, and a vivid suggestion of the body beneath (1.27). In the early fifth century BC there is a reaction and a return to a more severe style of drapery, one that covers and conceals and falls in heavy vertical folds again (1.28). By the end of the century, however, something more complex and decorative is once more in demand (1.29). A strong diagonal accent is again introduced in the drapery that slips off the shoulder and is, in terms of design, much like the cloak draped under the breast in figure 1.27 and several lively folds counteract the naturally simple vertical fall of the cloth; now too the body is again revealed. These swings in taste are virtually independent of the continuous progress in naturalistic representation.

TRENDS AND DEVELOPMENTS IN
ARCHAIC AND CLASSICAL STATUARY

Within a period of about two hundred years, we have seen a remarkable development in Greek sculpture from the earliest kouroi (1.1) to the classical perfection of the Spear-bearer (1.23). Acquiring the ability to imitate natural appearances was but one element in this complex evolution. Artists also had to find solutions to the unexpected problems that emerged, and to create works that embodied certain formal principles of design – through careful symmetrical patterning in the archaic period or by means of dynamic contrasts in the classical period. Finally, artists had to appreciate changes in taste: the way in which periods of delight in or rejection of the elaborate treatment of drapery alternated with one another.

Nature, design, fashion – all made demands on the sculptor. The factors that influenced the development of Greek art are many and complex. It would be unfair to the artists and to their achievements to simplify the situation in which they found themselves and the multitude of conditions they struggled so valiantly to satisfy.

2 Greek temples and their decoration

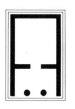

2.1a Plan of a simple temple consisting of just naos and pronaos.

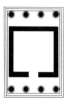

2.1b Plan of a temple with porches in front and at the back.

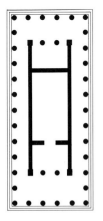

2.1c Plan of a temple with a peristyle.

The temple seems to us the most characteristic of all Greek buildings, and it would be natural to conclude that the Greeks regarded such buildings as a requirement for the worship of their gods and goddesses. In fact, nothing more than an open-air altar was really necessary. However, once the Greeks began to make statues of their deities, they had to provide a shelter to protect them and it was to serve this function that a temple was constructed. It was not built to accommodate a congregation, since religious ceremonies and rituals still took place at an altar outside the front (usually the east end) of the temple, and few people ever went inside.

A temple, whether made of wood or stone, could be very simple. A single room entered through a porch would suffice (2.1a). The room in which the statue of the god was kept was called a *naos* (the Romans called it a *cella*, and this term is sometimes also used of Greek temples). The porch was called a *pronaos* (literally, 'in front of the naos').

When a temple could easily be seen from more than one side, the Greeks disliked having the front and the back look different, so they added another porch at the rear (2.1b). There was usually no way into the temple from the back porch (called the *opisthodomos*); its only purpose was to give the temple a more symmetrical appearance.

This was how smaller temples were designed. Larger temples were built to stand free in a clear space so that they would be visible from many points of view and the Greeks tried to make all four sides of such temples look equally impressive by surrounding the core of the temple with a colonnade (2.1c, 2.2 and 2.3). This encircling colonnade was called a *peristyle* (from the Greek words *peri* 'around' and *stylos* 'column'), and it would usually contain the naos with its pronaos in front and the balancing opisthodomos behind (2.2).

The temple was generally built on a platform consisting of three

23

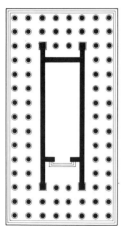

2.1d Plan of a temple with a double peristyle (dipteral).

steps. The top step was called the *stylobate* and on it stood the columns of the peristyle and the walls of the naos (2.3). Since a temple was part of a sanctuary, the entrance to the sanctuary would usually determine the angle from which the temple would first be seen. In most cases the approach gave on to a corner of the temple (see 6.5). From this angle (2.3), the temple could immediately be perceived as a three-dimensional volume rather than as a flat façade, and its principal dimensions (length, width, and height) could all be taken in at a glance. In its clarity, its independence, and its four equally satisfactory views, the peristyle temple is a characteristically Greek invention.

Some very rich poleis ostentatiously built temples with *two* sets of colonnades surrounding them. Such huge and costly structures must have looked very magnificent (2.1d).

The Greeks varied and modified their four fundamental plans for temples, making alterations in the proportions and the spacing of the elements from the time when they started building temples until the time when, with the triumph of Christianity, they stopped. Yet they kept the basic forms as constant as the pose of the kouros was kept throughout the archaic period. The Greeks liked to develop their ideas within a stable framework.

2.2   Plan of a typical peripteral temple.

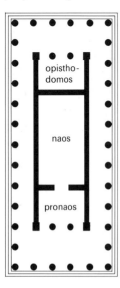

TWO BASIC ELEVATIONS: THE DORIC AND IONIC ORDERS

Greek temples were constructed on the simple post-and-lintel principle. Vertical posts (or columns or walls) supported horizontal lintels (or entablatures or ceilings). The earliest temples were built of wood and mud-brick on stone foundations. By the end of the seventh century BC, stone, which was both more expensive and more durable, began to be the preferred material for the building itself. The only temples of which substantial remains survive are those that were built of stone. In these, wall blocks were laid dry without any mortar. Coarse limestones were regularly coated with plaster to give them the appearance of an even surface. Marble was finely smoothed and so meticulously finished that the joins between one block and another are barely perceptible. Adjacent blocks were held in position chiefly by gravity, but some iron clamps sheathed in lead

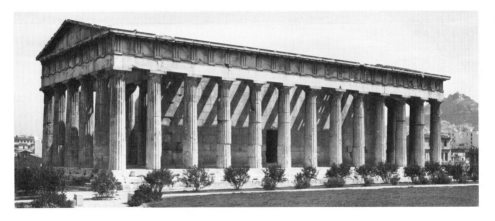

2.3   View of a peripteral Greek temple from a corner, third quarter of the 5th century BC, Hephaisteion, Athens.

were also used to keep them in place. These would not have been visible once the temple was completed. Columns were erected similarly, with wooden pins used to help centre one drum upon another and the joins were either so finely finished that they became virtually invisible or the whole was covered with a thin layer of plaster. In the final stages of building the columns were *fluted*, that is, vertical channels were carved in the shafts.

The columns supported a horizontal *entablature* comprising an *architrave* (a band of rectanglar blocks laid directly above the columns) that was surmounted by a *frieze*, and topped by a *cornice*. Both columns and entablatures were designed so that they belonged either to the *Doric* or to the *Ionic order*. In each order the proportions of all the elements and the scheme of decoration were coordinated with one another; mixing the two was rare before the Hellenistic period.

The Doric order (2.4) was strong, simple, and massive. The column *shafts* were sturdy (their height was only four to six times their lower diameters) and rested directly on the stylobate (2.3 and 2.7). The *capitals* surmounting the shafts were simple, cushion–like swellings topped by an undecorated square *abacus*, which supported a plain undivided architrave. This in turn supported the frieze which was divided into alternating *triglyphs* (vertically grooved rectangles whose appearance was reminiscent of beam ends) and *metopes* (rectangles which could be plain, painted, or sculpted in relief). There was one triglyph over each column and one between each pair of columns, so that the measured rhythm of the columns was exactly doubled in the rhythm of the frieze above (2.3).

The Ionic order (2.5) was more delicate and ornate. The column shafts were slender (ranging in height from eight to ten times their

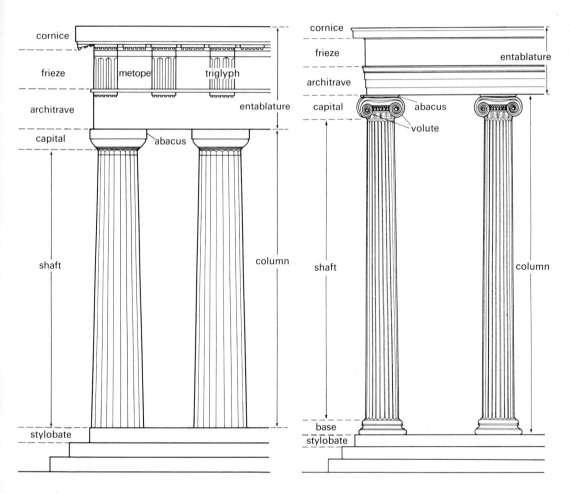

above
2.4   The Doric order.

above right
2.5   The Ionic order.

lower diameters) and rested on elaborate *bases* that consisted of at least two convex parts and one concave (2.5 and 2.6). Ionic capitals curve over to the right and left to end in *volutes* and are surmounted by a carved abacus, on which rests an architrave, often divided into three horizontal bands. The triple division subtly reflects the three steps on which the temple usually stands. The frieze above is undivided and may sometimes be decorated by a continuous band of relief carvings. The cornice at the top is richer than the Doric cornice and may carry several bands of pattern cut in relief.

The basic forms of the two orders were constant, but within limits the elements and proportions could be modified. The Ionic order was generally treated more freely than the Doric. For instance in the Ionic order as it first developed in the eastern Aegean and the coast of Asia Minor – and often later as well – *dentils* (small tooth-like carvings) were used at frieze level instead of a continuous frieze.

26

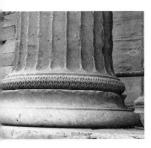

2.6 Base and bottom of the shaft of an Ionic column, late 5th century BC, Erechtheum, Athens.

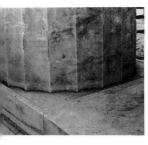

2.7 Bottom of the shaft of a Doric column, mid 5th century BC, Propylaea, Athens.

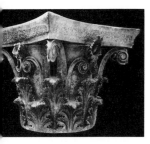

2.8 Corinthian capital, 4th century BC, Epidauros Museum.

And yet each order always preserved a special character of its own, so pervasive that it can be perceived even in details. Thus figure 2.7 conveys the strength and simplicity of the Doric order, while figure 2.6 reveals the grace and delicacy of the Ionic. (Both show the very bottom of a column – the shaft of the Doric and the base of the Ionic – where it rests on the stylobate.)

At the end of the fifth century BC, the Corinthian capital was invented (2.8). It soon became popular and was much used in Hellenistic and Roman times as an alternative to the Ionic capital within a somewhat enriched version of the Ionic order.

All temples were covered by a pitched roof, which left triangular gables at the front and back; these are called *pediments* (2.3). Decorative *acroteria* graced the three angles of the gables and softened the severe geometry of the temple's roof.

SPACES AND SHAPES TO DECORATE

Three areas on Greek temples invited sculpted (or painted) decoration; the triangular pediments on temples of either order (although those in the Ionic order were only seldom filled), the metopes on Doric temples, and the long, narrow, continuous friezes on Ionic temples.

None of these would have presented any problems if the Greeks had been content to fill them with floral or abstract patterns, as was sometimes done later by the Romans and eighteenth-century neo-classical decorators. But the Greeks were not satisfied with anything so simple. They wished instead to represent people, or monsters, and to represent them, if possible, enacting a story. Consider the problems that then arose.

PEDIMENTS AND THEIR PROBLEMS

A pediment is a long low triangle. It is not easy to arrange figures within it so that they will fill it harmoniously, tell a story, and tell it coherently. This is obvious from the difficulties encountered by the artist who carved huge figures in relief to decorate the pediment of

27

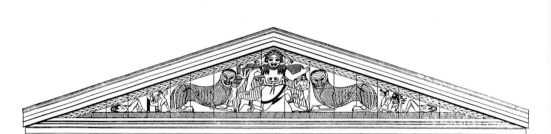

2.9   Reconstruction of
the west pediment of the
temple of Artemis on
Corfu, first quarter of the
6th century BC
(*c*. 580 BC).

the temple of Artemis in Corfu in the early years of the sixth century
BC (around 580) (2.9). The high centre of the triangle is filled by a
huge Gorgon, whose terrifying features would have been considered
effective in warding off evil spirits from the temple. But her role was
more than that of a mere guardian. This Gorgon was Medusa,
whose fate was to be decapitated by the hero Perseus. At the moment
of her death, she gave birth to two children, Pegasos the winged
horse and Chrysaor the man, who sprang from her neck as her head
was severed from it. Medusa, in her bent-knee pose, is meant to be
shown running away from Perseus; the unhappy outcome of her
flight is suggested by the presence of her two children, Pegasos on
the left, Chrysaor on the right.

The Gorgon is flanked on either side by crouching panthers.
They do not have her double function of simultaneously protecting
the temple and suggesting a story; they are just guardians of the
temple whose reclining posture enables them to fit comfortably into
the awkward slope of the pediment.

Tucked into the corners there are several tiny figures. These are
purely narrative. Those on the left come from the story of the fall of
Troy: King Priam, seated, is about to be killed by the Greek
attacking him; a dead Trojan lies behind him. The figures on the
right are participants in the battle of the gods and giants. The great
god Zeus, wielding his thunderbolt, has brought a giant to his knees.
Another giant lies supine in the corner.

Decoratively the pediment is superb; narratively it is incoherent.
Three completely unrelated stories are told, and they are told on
totally unrelated scales. This may not have been disturbing to
someone looking at the pediment at the time it was made. He might
have been pleased simply to recognize the three stories and to enjoy
each one in itself. He probably would not have thought of the
pediment space as a single field in which a unified image of reality
ought to appear. But demand for convincing and coherent representations, even within such an awkward triangular frame, did
eventually arise. This happened as a result of the way the Greeks

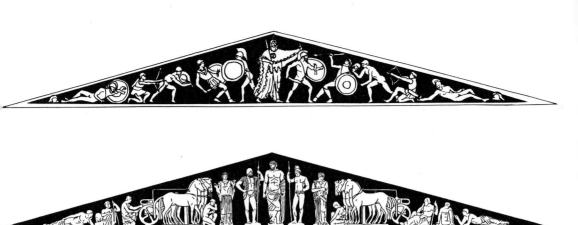

2.10 Reconstruction of
the east pediment of the
temple of Aphaia on
Aegina, first quarter of
the 5th century BC
(*c*. 490–480 BC).

2.11 Reconstruction of
the east pediment of the
temple of Zeus at
Olympia, second quarter
of the 5th century BC
(465–457 BC).

looked at art and of their notion, revolutionary at the time, that art
should be the mirror of nature.

We have seen that when the Greeks looked at the statue of a man,
they (unlike earlier peoples) thought of it more as a man than as a
statue. They therefore demanded that it should resemble a man, and
it was to meet this demand that increasingly naturalistic images were
produced. The Greeks thought about pediments similarly. At first
they were satisfied with a pleasant design and a multitude of stories,
but in time they came to think of the pediment shelf as a sort of stage
on which a plausible vision of a real situation should appear. Thus
they desired artists to fill the space of a pediment with a single story,
intelligibly told by figures all conceived on a single scale. This
presented a difficult problem, but within a century a satisfactory
solution had been devised.

The designer of the east pediment at Aegina, carved around 490
BC, chose to depict a mythological battle (2.10). It was a good choice.
The mighty goddess Athena stands in the centre, her helmeted head
reaching to the apex of the pediment. On either side mortal heroes,
who are naturally smaller than she, fight and fall, the incidents of
war being so arranged that those nearest the middle stand while
those further away stagger, lunge, crouch or lie, in conformity with
the slope of the pediment. The same scale is used for all the figures
(which are now carved fully in the round); the violent theme gives
plausibility to their different heights.

The next generation saw a *tour de force* in pedimental design: the
east pediment of the temple of Zeus at Olympia (465–457 BC) (2.11).
There is no violent action, and yet within a quiet scene a story is
compellingly told with figures of uniform scale, the whole pediment
being harmoniously filled.

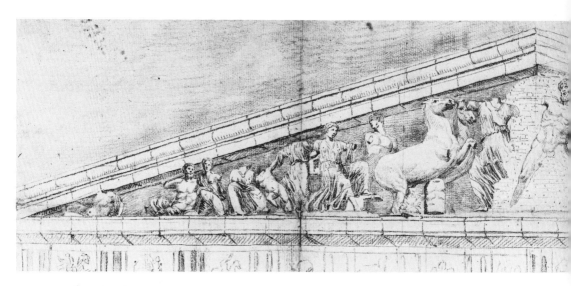

2.12 Seventeenth-
century drawing of the
west pediment of the
Parthenon in Athens,
third quarter of the 5th
century BC (438–432 BC),
drawing in the
Bibliothèque Nationale,
Paris.

In the centre stands Zeus, again the god who is taller than mere
men. On his right (our left) stands Oinomaos, king of Elis. He is
offering his daughter as bride to any man who can carry her off in his
chariot and reach the isthmus of Corinth before Oinomaos overtakes
and kills him. Oinomaos has divine horses, and twelve suitors have
already perished. A young man, modest in demeanour, stands to the
right listening. He is Pelops, destined to defeat the old king and
marry the girl. The prospective bride and her mother flank the men.
Next come the chariot teams; the horses' heads, since they are
higher than their rumps, are symmetrically turned towards the
centre. Behind them on one side squats a charioteer holding the
reins of the chariot and on the other a seer, dismayed, is seated
peering into the future where he witnesses the terrible disaster in
store for Oinomaos. Servants and other subordinate characters sit
near the corners which are neatly filled with reclining river gods,
their legs extending into the furthest angles (2.20).

The scene is tense, unified, and effective. The subtle difference in
the characterizations of the arrogant Oinomaos and the modest
Pelops, the intense involvement of the principal characters and the
detachment of the servants – one boy passing the time absent-
mindedly playing with his toes – is part of the early classical
exploration of personality and mood which we also saw in the
Kritios boy (1.10 and 1.14) and the Zeus of Artemisium (1.15 and
1.16).

The pediments of the Parthenon in Athens, carved a generation
later (438–432 BC), are even more ambitious. The temple was

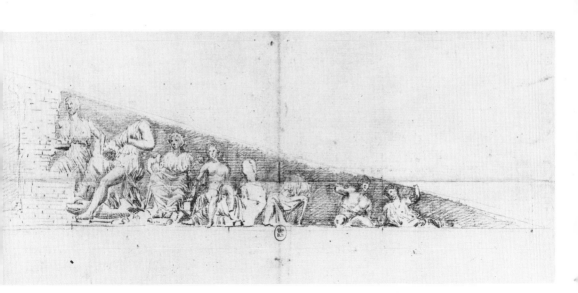

unusually broad and so the pediments had to be extraordinarily
wide, a change in scale that intensified the problems inherent in
pediment design. While the pediments at Olympia were comfortably filled with about fifteen figures, well over twenty were required
to fill the pediments of the Parthenon. Since these were placed
higher up from the ground than usual, they were deeply carved so
that they would catch the light and remain intelligible at a distance.
Though they are boldly designed, these figures are finished with
great refinement (2.21) and even the backs, which would not have
been visible once they were in place, have been completed with
scrupulous care.

The west pediment showed the contest of the goddess Athena and
the god Poseidon for the patronage of Athens (2.12). The two huge
deities occupied the centre, pulling away from each other. Teams of
horses probably reared up on either side. We have to rely on a
seventeenth-century drawing for our information about the design,
as most of the sculpture still visible then has since been destroyed.
From the violent thrusts and counterthrusts in the middle of the
pediment, waves of excitement eddy out, finally coming to rest in
the calm and unconcerned reclining figures of the river gods at the
corners.

The river god (2.21) that once occupied the left corner of the west
pediment and now can be found in the British Museum illustrates
the combination of grandeur and subtlety that distinguishes the
pedimental sculpture of the Parthenon. Muscles flex, flow, and
ripple, while the relaxed belly gently sags forward. Anatomy is

portrayed naturalistically but without finicky detail. The softness of flesh, the strength of muscle, the hardness of bone are all suggested but not exhaustively explored.

The sense of drama and excitement in this pediment is marvellously conveyed (2.12), but beyond the striking central composition, things seem to fall to pieces almost as they did in the Corfu pediment (2.9). The gods and goddesses at the sides witnessing the spectacular event taking place in their midst are very shrunken in scale. Notice how tiny the river god in the corner is compared with Poseidon in the centre. As far as design is concerned, the artist has overreached himself and has tried to accommodate too many figures. The dazzling brilliance of the carving of the few surviving figures has, however, tended to divert attention from the imperfections of the composition.

METOPES: FEW BUT TELLING FIGURES

Metopes, being nearly square, are easier to decorate and fill than pediments. If, however, the artist wants the story presented in a metope to be intelligible at a distance, he must carefully choose the moment to be illustrated and use no more than three or four figures.

The sculptor of a metope on the treasury of the Sicyonians at Delphi, carved around 560 BC, has produced a fine piece of decoration (2.13). (A treasury was a small building erected in a panhellenic sanctuary to hold the dedications and offerings made by the polis that built it.) The metope now shows three heroes – originally there was at least one more – marching off to the right proudly accompanying the oxen they have stolen in a cattle raid. They occupy the full height of the metope, a triad of parallel vertical figures. They hold their sloping spears at the same angle and walk in step with the cattle, whose legs, meticulously aligned, recede into the background of the relief. A fine pattern emerges, elegantly composed of repeated shapes in the archaic manner (cf. 1.5).

The metopes on the outside of the temple of Zeus at Olympia (465–457 BC) were left plain, but the twelve metopes over the porches, six over the front porch and six over the back, were carved

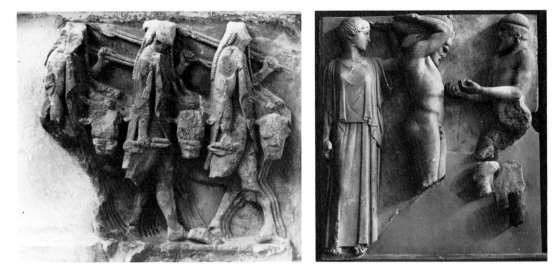

in relief. They illustrated the twelve labours of Herakles, one labour
to each metope.

One labour required Herakles to fetch the apples of immortality
from the garden of the Hesperides. Herakles persuaded Atlas to
bring the apples to him while he held up the heavens in Atlas' place
(2.14). The metope shows Atlas, rejoicing in his unusual freedom of
movement, striding to the left holding the apples in his outstretched
hands. Herakles faces him, oppressed by the burden that rests
heavily on his shoulders. The goddess Athena, his protectress,
stands on the far left, one hand raised in an easy gesture of aid to the
hero.

Something subtler than the parallel lines and repeated patterns
on the metope from the Sicyonian treasury (2.13) relates the three
figures on the Olympia metope (2.14). Atlas, the only figure shown
in action, moves in from the right. His chest is shown in three-
quarter front view; his extended forearms make a strong horizontal
contrast with the predominant verticals of the design and draw our
attention to the apples in his hands. Profile to profile he meets
Herakles, who is shown in side view. Athena, majestic and still,
brings the movement to an end. The metope was the last of the
series on the left and her vertical figure, fully frontal, gives finality
to the total design. Athena's sympathy with Herakles is delicately
indicated, not only by her upraised hand, but also by the turn of her
head – in profile, like Herakles, confronting Atlas.

The master of the Olympia metopes could also portray conflict
superbly. He showed Herakles fighting the monstrous Cretan bull

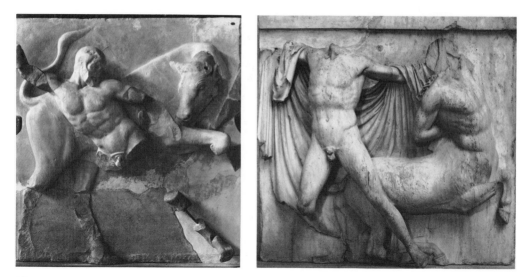

above
2.15 Herakles and the Cretan bull, metope from the temple of Zeus at Olympia, *c.* 460 BC, height 160 cm, Louvre, Paris.

above right
2.16 Lapith and centaur, metope from the Parthenon in Athens, 447–442 BC, height 134 cm, British Museum, London.

(2.15) as a composition based on two crossing diagonals, so that both figures could appear especially large in relation to those on the other metopes. In a splendid invention designed to convey the intensity of the struggle, he makes the hero wrench the head of the gigantic bull round to confront him face to face.

The dynamism of this explosive composition was much appreciated in later times. The same structure underlies the conflict of the central figures in the west pediment of the Parthenon (2.12) and it was also used for one of the most striking metopes on the Parthenon (2.16).

The Parthenon was exceptionally richly decorated with architectural sculpture. Not only were the unusually wide pediments crammed with figures, but also all ninety-two of the metopes on the outside of the temple were carved (in 447–442 BC). Those on the south, almost the only ones reasonably well preserved, represented the conflict of the Lapiths with the centaurs, mythical creatures that were part man and part horse. In one metope (2.16) man and monster pull energetically away from one another; the tense struggle is visually accentuated by the play of light and shadow on the deep folds of the cloak that falls behind the Lapith and over his arms. The Lapith's body is rendered by such a subtle wealth of anatomical detail and by transitions of so great a delicacy and softness as to make the Olympia metopes with their grand simplifications look, by contrast, ruggedly severe.

The metope at the western end of the south side of the Parthenon is magnificent (2.17). Like the Olympia metope showing Herakles

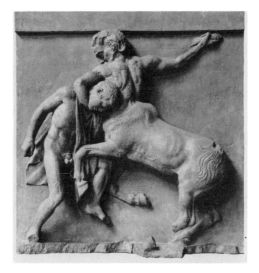

2.17   Lapith and centaur, metope at the western end of the south side of the Parthenon (from a cast), 447–442 BC, height 134 cm.

receiving the apples of the Hesperides (2.14), it was the last metope on the left of a series. Whereas the still figure of Athena terminates the movement at Olympia, the action in the Parthenon metope is closed by the vigorous curve of the body of the Lapith as he thrusts a spit, which was originally added in bronze, into the side of the attacking centaur. The same artistic purpose is served, but with greater freedom.

From the schematic, handsomely patterned design of the archaic metope on the treasury of the Sicyonians (2.13), the Greeks gradually evolved the dynamic, classical balance of the finest metopes of the Parthenon (2.16 and 2.17).

FRIEZES: DIFFICULTIES OF DESIGN

Friezes presented more problems of design than metopes. A frieze was an immensely long, narrow ribbon for which it was not easy to find a satisfactory subject. The elaborate decoration of the Parthenon included a frieze, which was an unusual Ionic feature in this predominantly Doric temple. It was carved between 442 and 438 BC (2.18 and 2.19 and 7.6). The theme chosen was a procession in honour of the goddess Athena. It is designed so that the participants in the sculpted frieze appear to accompany the observer walking along beside the temple in the same direction. On three sides the procession all moves in one direction for the whole length of the side (2.18). At the front the two arms of the procession converge towards

35

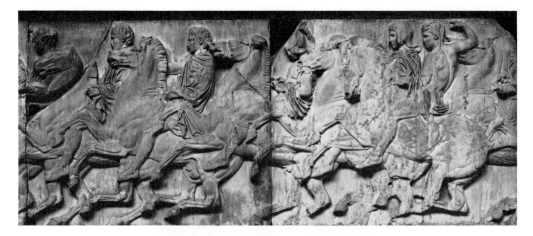

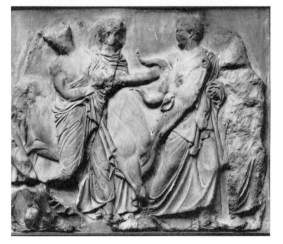

above
2.18 Part of the procession on the Parthenon frieze, 442–438 BC, height 106 cm, British Museum, London.

right
2.19 Part of the procession on the Parthenon frieze, 442–438 BC, height 106 cm, British Museum, London.

the centre, producing a natural point of rest for the eye. The flow of the figures is unified but not monotonous. Sometimes the procession is dense and the figures move along quickly (2.18); at other times the pace is measured (2.19) or even stately (7.6).

THE EARLY AND HIGH CLASSICAL STYLES CONTRASTED

The exquisite carving of the frieze of the Parthenon is revealed by a detail of some youths bringing a heifer to sacrifice (2.19). The austere simplicity of the Olympia metope (2.15) looks almost harsh in comparison with the richly expressive carving on the Parthenon frieze. Notice how differently the heifer is rendered from the Cretan bull. The same contrast can be seen in a comparison between a river

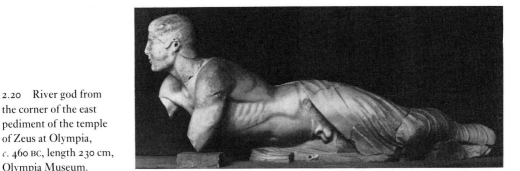

2.20 River god from
the corner of the east
pediment of the temple
of Zeus at Olympia,
c. 460 BC, length 230 cm,
Olympia Museum.

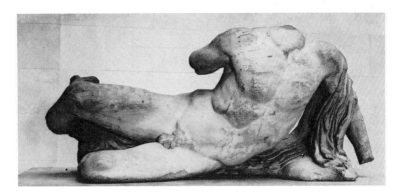

2.21 River god from
the west pediment of the
Parthenon in Athens,
438–432 BC, length
156 cm, British
Museum, London.

god from the east pediment at Olympia (2.20) and a river god from
the west pediment of the Parthenon (2.21).

An observer living in ancient times who could have compared the
original early-classical Discus-thrower (1.18) with the original high-
classical Spear-bearer (1.23) would have noticed a similar contrast.
The two works must have differed not only in design but also in style
and the treatment of the surface. The severe simplicity of Myron's
conception affected every aspect of his statue; the delicate balance of
forms in the stance of the Spear-bearer was symptomatic of
Polykleitos' method of working; he was particularly celebrated for
the refinement of his finish. If we combine in our minds the design of
the Discus-thrower with the austere vitality of the Olympia
sculptures and the poise of the Spear-bearer with the delicacy of
surface of the Parthenon sculptures, we will come close to appreciat-
ing why the achievements of the early-classical and the high-
classical periods were so much admired.

3 Painting and painted pottery

PAINTING ON WALLS AND PANELS

below

3.1 Perseus fleeing with the Gorgon's head, painted metope from the temple of Apollo at Thermon, second half of the 7th century BC, height 88 cm, water-colour (original in the National Archaeological Museum, Athens).

below right

3.2 Copy of painted wooden panel from Pitsa near Corinth, second half of the 6th century BC, height 14.5 cm, National Archaeological Museum, Athens.

The Greeks, like us, thought of painting primarily in terms of paintings on walls and panels. Large paintings on flat surfaces were often used to decorate architecture; metopes, for instance, would sometimes be painted rather than carved in relief. Figure 3.1 shows a seventh-century-BC example from Thermon. The metope is about a metre square and depicts the hero Perseus, who, having beheaded the fierce Gorgon and put her terrifying head in a bag (the eyes can be seen peering out), runs off to the right. The pin-wheel form of the figure in flight is well conceived to fill the whole surface of the metope in a decorative and lively way. The metope is made of terracotta and painted in black and shades of red and orange, colours that were suitable for firing. There is no effort to show the figure realistically in space; this is just a fine pattern, recognizable as a running man, arranged to make a handsome decoration.

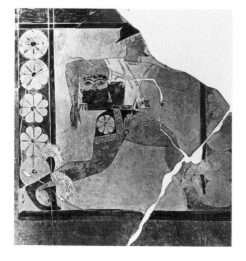

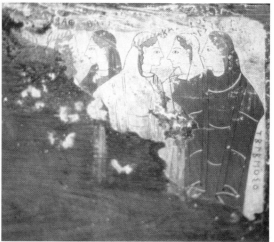

This is practically the only well-preserved example we have of large-scale painting from this period.

The Greeks also painted on wooden panels. In figure 3.2 several women are shown chatting: their delicate profiles are outlined in red. Reds and blues are freely used for clothing. This is an exquisite piece of drawing. It is still very flat, but the overlapping of one figure on top of another suggests the existence of the figures in space. The panel was painted in the later sixth century BC. Wood decays in the Greek climate, and this panel and the others found with it at Pitsa near Corinth are virtually the only paintings on wood to survive to the present day.

If we had to learn about Greek painting from examples such as these, we would have very little to go on. Fortunately we have another source of information: pottery. In most civilizations pottery decoration is a minor art, sometimes attractive but usually unimportant. This was not so with the Greeks, at least not until the dawn of the classical period.

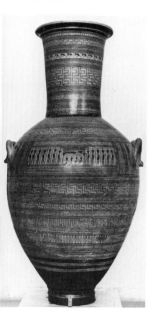

3.3 Amphora showing mourners around a bier, mid 8th century BC, height 155 cm, National Archaeological Museum, Athens.

PAINTINGS ON POTTERY: THE BEGINNING

Decorating a pot is a very different matter from painting a picture on a flat surface. The outer surfaces of the pot are rounded and parts curve away from the viewer. The profile can be strangely irregular; the outline of a pot (for instance 3.3) can sometimes even look like an inverted keyhole. This would make an oddly shaped frame for an ordinary picture. Of course the Greeks did not use the contour of a pot as a frame for a picture but skilfully adjusted their designs to the vessels they were ornamenting.

Even as early as the eighth century BC, while the Homeric epics were being formulated, grand and impressive pieces of pottery could be created. Though the pot shown in 3.3 is huge, about a metre and a half high, the elements that decorate it are small. They cover the surface with a network of light and dark, subtly varied to emphasize the different structural parts of the vessel: off-set lip, cylindrical neck, expanding shoulder, wide belly, and tapering foot. Strong triads of horizontal lines divide the surface into bands. All the patterns within the bands (except for the three that are decorated

39

amphora

hydria

krater

oinochoe

kylix

skyphos

with living creatures, namely the grazing deer and reclining goats on the neck and the men on the belly) are designed to be either vertical or horizontal. In this way the decoration is made to enhance the stable and monumental appearance of the vessel and to contrast piquantly with its curving contour.

Human figures appear only in one small but important section: the panel between the two handles. They are slim, elegant stick figures painted in flat silhouette. The scene represents mourners around a bier. The whole gigantic piece of pottery was used as a grave marker, and the sombre, controlled, meticulous decoration accords well with this function.

Pottery had been briefly elevated to the status of a monumental art, but from the end of the seventh century BC on, stone slabs (*stelai*, singular: *stele*) that were either painted or carved in relief – or even statues in the round, like kouroi – were used as grave markers, and pottery went back to functioning as the useful craft it had always been.

HOW GREEK POTTERY WAS USED

The Greeks made pots with painted decoration to serve four main purposes (3.4):

1. *As containers and storage jars of ample capacity in which wine, water, olive oil and dry goods were kept*: a pot with two handles is called an *amphora*; one with three handles (two at the sides for lifting and one at the back for pouring) used for water is called a *hydria*.

2. *As equipment for drinking parties*: the Greeks drank their wine diluted with water; they therefore needed a wide-mouthed mixing bowl called a *krater* into which they could pour the two liquids, and a jug called an *oinochoe* to dip it out so that it could be poured into a delicate cup (*kylix*) or a more humble mug (*skyphos*).

3. *As vessels used in connection with personal adornment*: olive oil was very important in Greek life, not only for cooking, but also for lighting, for cleaning the body, and as a base for perfumes. A *lekythos* could hold as much as a litre or two of olive oil and had a narrow neck to restrict the flow. An *alabastron* was a small flask with a very constricted neck from which a lady could shake a few drops of

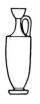

lekythos

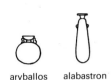

aryballos   alabastron

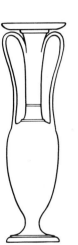

loutrophoros

perfume. Still smaller and rather rounder was an *aryballos*, a vessel equipped with a thong for carrying or hanging which was used by men to hold the olive oil they used to rub down with after exercise.

4. *As special vessels for use in rituals*: for instance the *loutrophoros* was used to carry the water for a bride's ritual bath before her wedding. Sometimes a stone model of a loutrophoros was placed on the grave of an unmarried person. Olive oil was often presented to the dead in a lekythos covered with a white slip and fugitive paint that would have been unsuitably delicate for everyday use. Such *white-ground lekythoi* were occasionally made with false necks so that only a small part at the top had to be filled to give the impression that the whole vessel was full, a clever bit of economizing.

In the eighteenth century, when the modern study of ancient pottery began, all these vessels were called 'vases'. This conventional designation has persisted ever since, despite the fact that Greek pottery was clearly made to serve a purely utilitarian function, was only incidentally used as decoration, and almost never held cut flowers.

NEW INTERESTS IN THE SEVENTH CENTURY BC

By the seventh century BC human figures and their activities had become for artists in several areas of Greece the most important part of the vase painting. Homer's poems were by then very popular and the vase painter longed to follow the poet's example and himself become a story-teller (3.5). He therefore simplified the traditional patterned decoration and banished most of it to the bottom of the vase, thus clearing the principal area of his krater for the presentation of an exciting tale. From this time on, vase painters, like the artists who later carved architectural sculptures, strove to show men (and monsters) in action. Greek mythology was rich in tales of adventure – Homer recounted some of them in the *Iliad* and the *Odyssey* – and they provided an unending source of inspiration for artists.

The story represented here is taken from the ninth book of the *Odyssey*, which described how Odysseus and his men were trapped in the cave of the terrible man-eating, one-eyed Cyclops. The

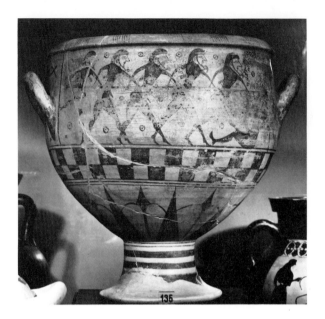

3.5 Krater by Aristonothos showing Odysseus and his friends blinding the Cyclops, mid 7th century BC, height 36 cm, Museo dei Conservatori, Rome.

Cyclops closed the mouth of the cave with an enormous boulder, too large for the men to move. Even if they had succeeded in killing the Cyclops they would have perished, trapped in the cave. Ingenious Odysseus realized this and so devised a way to blind the monster, get the Cyclops to move the boulder himself and then slip out of the cave, with his men, undetected.

The painted scene shows Odysseus and his men, having got the Cyclops drunk, driving a great stake into his single eye. The men are drawn in flat silhouette, except for their faces which are in outline. The Cyclops, who looks a bit small for a giant, sits on the ground to the right.

The artist has had to try to satisfy two rather contradictory conditions: to decorate his vase with an effective pattern and to make his story clearly intelligible. He has succeeded in telling the story with great liveliness and has, at the same time, made the repeated forms of the men working in unison into a pleasing pattern. And yet this bold decoration seems less perfectly suited to the shape of the vessel than that used on the earlier monumental vase (3.3).

We happen to know who made this vase (3.5), for Aristonothos was one of the first potters to put his name on his work. From now on potters and painters somewhat irregularly sign their work. Many of the best artists, however, never signed at all, and even good artists, whose signatures we know, could leave their finest works unsigned.

VIVIDNESS IN STORY-TELLING:
THE BLACK-FIGURE TECHNIQUE

Story-telling eventually came to be the overwhelming concern of the painters who decorated vases. It captivated and enthralled them; other considerations became largely subordinate. It provided a powerful impetus toward naturalism, for painters were constantly looking for ways to make their stories livelier and more convincing. They felt that the vividness of Homeric poetry was a challenge to them and tried to rival it; they, too, wished to make stories come alive for their audiences.

It was difficult for painters to achieve this new goal while working just with silhouettes. Most stories required figures to interact and overlap, but the overlapping of silhouettes could only lead to confusion. Some painters, therefore, briefly experimented with outlining their figures. Unfortunately the outlines looked disappointingly thin on the burnished curving surface of a pot. The conflicting demands of persuasive narration and effective decoration stimulated the search for a better solution.

The solution came with the invention of the black-figure technique. The artist first painted his figures in silhouette so that they would look bold and telling, then he incised their contours and inner markings with a sharp instrument that removed the paint along the line of incision and left the outlines clear. He also added touches of white and purplish-red so that the scenes became more colourful. Since the added white and purplish-red proved less durable than the black paint and the basic orange of the background, on many black-figure vases little trace of them remains.

The vase painter Kleitias obtained wonderful effects with the black-figure technique around 570–560 BC (3.6). The picture of Ajax carrying the dead body of his friend Achilles is part of the decoration of the handle of a particularly richly painted krater (the so-called François vase). An extremely moving image has been created. The great hero Ajax rises with difficulty under the burden of the even greater hero whom he lifts. The body of Achilles is draped limply over the shoulders of his friend. The arms drop lifelessly; the hair hangs heavily. Notice the closed eye of the dead Achilles and how it contrasts with the wide-open, sorrowful eye of

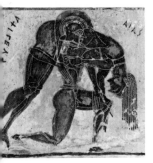

3.6 Black-figured painting by Kleitias of Ajax carrying the body of Achilles on the handle of a krater (the 'François vase'), *c.* 570–560 BC, Museo Archeologico, Florence.

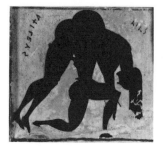

above
3.7 Drawing of 3.6
without the incision.

right
3.8 Black-figured
amphora made and
painted by Exekias
showing Ajax and
Achilles playing a game,
c. 540–530 BC, height
61 cm, Vatican Museum,
Rome.

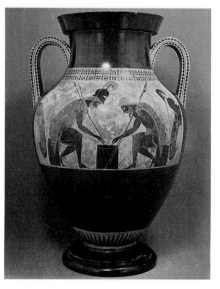

Ajax. Achilles was a fast runner (Homer calls him 'swift-footed Achilles'), but death has extinguished his speed. Kleitias recalls what Achilles was in life; look how carefully he has drawn the kneecaps and how he has indicated the strong muscles in the legs. Figure 3.7 shows how unintelligible this picture would be if attempted in silhouette alone. The incised lines that articulate the image are obviously essential.

A generation later, in the third quarter of the sixth century BC, there lived the greatest of all black-figure masters: Exekias. A good example of the exquisite refinement of his style is the picture he painted on an amphora (3.8) showing Ajax and Achilles playing a game, the same two heroes we saw painted by Kleitias, but here in a happier moment. The heroes' finely embroidered cloaks are rendered by means of the most delicate incision. The serene composition captures the tranquillity of the scene and the absorption of the heroes. As they bend towards the gaming board, the curve of their backs echoes the curve of the amphora. Exekias shows that he was very much aware that he was decorating a vase. Not only does he make the outlines of the heroes follow the outlines of the vessel, but he also places the spears so that they lead the eye up to the top of the handles, and arranges the shields behind the heroes so that they continue the vertical line formed by the lower part of the handles.

The stature of Exekias becomes very clear if one compares his amphora with one done by another, lesser artist (3.9) who has taken over the theme, and to a large extent also the composition, from Exekias. The differences are marked: only the shield and spears of

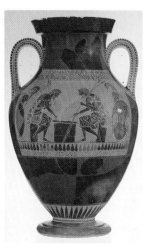

3.9 Black-figured drawing on an amphora showing Ajax and Achilles playing a game, *c.* 530–520 BC, height 55 cm, Museum of Fine Arts, Boston.

the left-hand hero relate to the shape of the vessel; the embroidery on the cloaks is simpler; neither hero wears a helmet and so the composition lacks unity and tends to fall apart into two virtually symmetrical halves. Still, this is a good artist; it is only that his painting lacks that genius which makes Exekias' work so outstanding.

THE SEARCH FOR NEW EFFECTS: THE RED-FIGURE TECHNIQUE

Exekias used the black-figure technique so brilliantly and so imaginatively that other gifted artists might have felt that he left them nothing to improve on. Possibly this is why a pupil of Exekias' decided to try something different (3.10). What he did was simply reverse the traditional colour scheme and instead of painting black figures on an orange-red ground, he left the figures in the natural colour of the clay and painted the background black. For painters this new red-figure technique had many advantages. It preserved the strong decorative contrast of the colours unchanged but it gave greater scope for drawing, since a supple brush could be used instead of a harsh engraving tool. Anatomy became livelier, cloth softer, and the figures more vibrant with life.

3.10 Red-figured drawing on an amphora showing Ajax and Achilles playing a game (the other side of 3.9).

The red-figure technique was invented around 530 BC and was quickly taken up by the best and most ambitious painters, although mediocre painters continued working in black-figure until the middle of the fifth century BC. The older technique was used for special purposes right up until the second century BC, but it had lost its fascination.

Euthymides, working in the last decade of the sixth century BC, was delighted with the facility that red-figure gave him. Like artists carving reliefs at that time and also those doing free painting (as we learn from ancient writers), Euthymides was much concerned with the problems of three-dimensional representation, that is, with showing full, round figures, convincingly rendered by means of foreshortening (3.11). To explore these effects he hardly needed to illustrate a story; scenes from everyday life were just as good. These had formed only a minor current in black-figure painting. On the amphora illustrated (3.11), he shows three drunken revellers

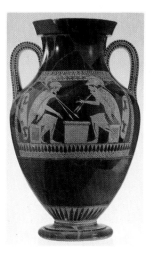

45

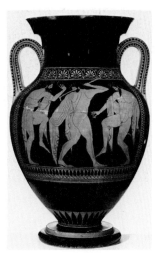

3.11 Red-figured
amphora painted by
Euthymides showing
revellers, *c.* 510–500 BC,
height 60 cm, Staatliche
Antikensammlungen
und Glyptothek,
Munich.

carousing. The central one is the most striking. He is drawn from the back, a novel point of view. Euthymides was so pleased with this work that he wrote on the vase 'Euphronios [a rival painter] never did anything so good': a proud boast, for the works by Euphronios that we know are powerful indeed. This remark gives us a vivid insight into the lively competition between artists that spurred them on to face and overcome ever new problems.

No one at the time could have challenged the inventiveness and excellence of Euthymides' drawing, nor could anyone have failed to marvel at the way he suggested the massiveness and volume of his figures. The surface of the amphora has been transformed into a field for the exhibition of advances in foreshortening; for the best artists there could now be no turning back. And yet, was it appropriate to decorate the curving surface of a vase in this way? Are not plain silhouettes, or even the highly elaborated silhouettes of Exekias (3.8), more suitable? Regarded purely as applied decoration, is not the geometric vase (3.3) the most satisfying? Perhaps, as we have seen before, progress in one direction (naturalistic drawing) has produced problems in another (decorative effectiveness).

By the beginning of the fifth century BC the red-figure technique had been thoroughly mastered. Now it could be used expressively, as is shown in a painting on a hydria that depicts the mythological sack of Troy (3.12). The old king Priam sits on an altar – this ought to have assured him of divine protection, but an arrogant young warrior grasps him by the shoulder to steady the old man as he prepares, heartlessly, to deliver the death blow. King Priam puts his hands to his head. It is less a gesture of self-protection than a gesture of despair. His grandson, brutally murdered, lies on his lap, the child's body gashed with horrible wounds. How different this scene of the death of Priam is from the crude and simple image on the Corfu pediment (2.9)!

Another part of the painting shows a Greek warrior harshly pulling a woman away from the statue of a goddess to which she clings for protection. Notice the eloquence of the pleading hand she extends towards him. Old men, children, defenceless women: these are the ones that suffer in war. The artist knew it well. He was an Athenian living at the time of the Persian wars.

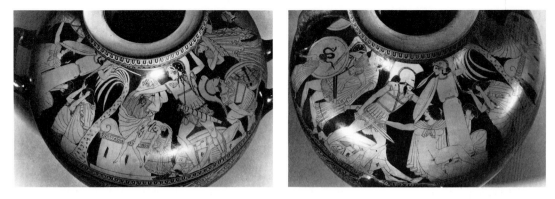

3.12   Red-figured
hydria shoulder showing
the fall of Troy,
c. 490–480 BC, total
height 42 cm, Museo
Nazionale, Naples.

ADVANCES IN WALL PAINTING: POLYGNOTOS

The most famous artist in the quarter-century following the Persian
wars, the early classical period (about 475–450 BC), was the painter
Polygnotos. He was a mural painter and none of his works survive,
but from what ancient writers tell us and from imitations and
adaptations of his and his contemporaries' work in sculpture and
vase painting, we can get some idea of what his revolutionary
paintings must have been like.

Polygnotos was most interested in the delineation of human
character, and this he did through quiet and intense scenes. The
still, tense, expressive group of figures in the east pediment at
Olympia (2.11) with their sensitively rendered, contrasting personalities shows profound influence from Polygnotos. Something of
his special quality can also be seen echoed in a painting on a krater
which shows Orpheus, the legendary musician who could charm
animals and stones and even the gods of the Underworld with his
songs, playing to four Thracian listeners (3.13). The characters of
the four and their attitudes toward the spellbinding music are all
finely differentiated. The youth to the left of the singer has yielded
entirely. He closes his eyes and listens enraptured. His companion
(far left) leans on his shoulder and gazes dreamily at the singer. The
two men at the right seem less well-disposed towards music. The
one closest to Orpheus stares intently at him, angrily trying to
fathom the power of his art. The one on the far right is thoroughly
disapproving and turns to leave (notice his feet); but he looks back.
He cannot break the spell. Orpheus himself, absorbed in his song,
belongs to a wholly different realm.

Such a static scene works well in a small panel on a vase, but
Polygnotos decorated great walls with huge compositions filled with

47

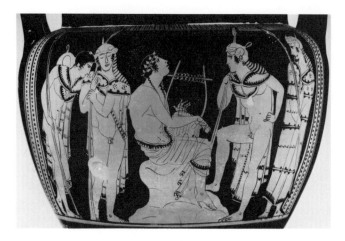

3.13 Red-figured krater showing Orpheus playing to the Thracians, *c.* 440 BC, height 51 cm, Antikenmuseum, Staatliche Museen Preussischer Kulturbesitz, W. Berlin.

many figures. Depictions of action make for exciting arrangements, but since Polygnotos wished to reveal character through quietly standing figures, he had to devise a different way of making his compositions lively. What he did was to distribute his figures up and down the wall at different levels so as to cover the surface with interesting groups. A possibly unexpected consequence of this innovation was that the figures higher up looked as if they were farther away, that is, the figures appeared to be receding behind each other and the wall itself ceased to appear entirely flat but began to suggest an indefinite space.

It is unlikely that Polygnotos greatly diminished the scale of his apparently more distant figures and probable that he set his scene on a hillside so that a certain ambiguity between higher up and farther away would blunt the impact of his daring novelty. For what his paintings threatened to do was to pierce a hole in the wall they decorated, and that must have been a startling, even alarming, idea when it first arose.

A few vase painters tried to copy Polygnotan compositions (3.14). It was a mistake. The shiny black background negates the suggestion of space and the scatter of figures looks odd and purposeless. Now for the first time vase painting and free painting go their separate ways.

THE ILLUSION OF SPACE

We take it for granted that three-dimensional objects and three-dimensional space can be represented on a flat surface; illusionistic

48

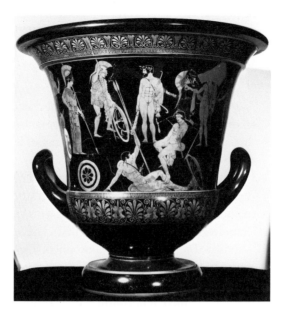

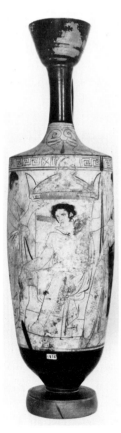

pictures are part of our everyday experience. Before the Greeks, they did not exist. The Greeks invented them.

Euthymides (3.11) and his contemporaries in the late sixth century BC began using foreshortening in their drawing of individual figures in order to give them the appearance of being three-dimensional. By the end of the fifth century BC the painter Parrhasios had become so accomplished in this technique that he was supposed to have been able to draw outlines so suggestive that they seemed to reveal even what was concealed. This he seems to have done without the aid of internal markings or shading. Something of his achievement may be reflected in a white-ground lekythos that was used as a funeral offering (3.15) which shows striking economy of line and spareness of internal marking combined with an impressive suggestion of volume.

Zeuxis, a contemporary of Parrhasios, was also concerned with making his figures appear to have mass. He chose to do so not through suggestive outline but through the clever use of shading. His was the approach that captured the imagination of later painters. Parrhasios' immense skill in drawing was much valued, and examples of his work were treasured for centuries, but it was Zeuxis' more painterly method of indicating volume by means of modelling that was developed further. Still later, painters began to study the effects of highlights and reflected light.

Massive bodies seem to exist in their own space. When they are

shown overlapping, the space is deepened, and when some are
shown higher than others, as in Polygnotos' paintings, there is some
hint of the existence of space itself and of the fact that figures are set
into it.

The idea of creating a sense of space in its own right seems to have
been explored during the later fifth century BC by Agatharchos, who
painted stage sets. His experiments with vanishing points (receding
lines in architectural drawings that converge at a point) apparently
stimulated contemporary philosophers (Democritos and Anaxagoras)
to make a theoretical study of perspective. Such, at any rate, is the
testimony of Vitruvius (VII.xi), one of the writers from whose works
we derive much of our information about classical painting.

WRITTEN SOURCES OF INFORMATION ON THE ARTS

Vitruvius lived in the time of the Roman emperor Augustus (31
BC–AD 14) and wrote a book about the theory and practice of
architecture. From time to time, almost in asides, he says something
about painting. Other authors such as Plutarch (who wrote
biographies), Aristotle (who wrote a criticism of poetry), Cicero (the
Roman orator, who also wrote philosophical treatises) or Lucian
(who composed witty satires) also mention Greek painters and
painting. From these incidental remarks we can learn a great deal.

Two ancient writers, however, stand apart from the rest, for they
give us more than just snatches of information.

The first is Pliny. He was a Roman polymath, interested in
everything. (The breadth of his intellectual curiosity finally killed
him, for he died while he was investigating the cataclysmic eruption
of Vesuvius in AD 79.) He wrote an encyclopaedic book, *Natural
History*, which was a descriptive work divided into sections on
animals, vegetables and minerals. In part of the section about
minerals he dealt with the stones and metals used by sculptors and
some of the pigments used by painters that are made from minerals,
and this led him to give a short history of sculpture and painting.
Pliny discussed the development of the arts, the contributions of
different artists, and some individual celebrated works.

The second major source of information is Pausanias. He was

a Greek traveller who lived in the second century AD and wrote a guide to Greece addressed to the tourists of his time. He walked through the most important cities and sanctuaries in mainland Greece, noting things of interest and describing the famous works of art that he saw. He devoted long passages to paintings by Polygnotos and it was from studying his detailed descriptions that modern scholars realized that Polygnotos set some figures higher than others and were able to recognize that kraters like figure 3.14 were reflections of his work.

Such authors also tell us a great deal about sculpture. Much of the information they set down comes from Greek sources going back at least as early as the fourth century BC. By then the Greeks had realized that in their art they had created something entirely new and noteworthy and were eager to comment upon it. Even as far back as the sixth century BC, some architects had written books about their work, and we know that the sculptor Polykleitos in the fifth century BC wrote a treatise explaining the principles on which he made his Spear-bearer. Actual histories of art were written in the fourth century BC, and many anecdotes were recorded about artists. Unfortunately most of this material is lost but the fragments that are preserved, embedded in the works of Pliny, Pausanias and other authors, give us valuable insights we could not obtain elsewhere.

Even so we learn disappointingly little about the lives and personalities of archaic and classical artists. Myron was famous in his time, but Pliny (*Natural History* 34.57–8) only tells us where he was born and who his teacher was, enumerates his best-known works, and makes a few general remarks on his style. Lucian's detailed description of Myron's Discus-thrower '. . . who is bent over into the throwing position, is turned toward the hand that holds the discus and has the opposite knee gently flexed, like one who will straighten up again after the throw . . .' (*Philopseudes* 18) enables us to recognize Roman copies of this work (1.18). But other master-pieces, like the Zeus of Artemisium (1.16), cannot with certainty be ascribed to any artist we know of, while many of the names recorded by ancient authorities cannot be related to any works that survive either in the original or in copies.

The fragments of information that we can glean from literary sources are sometimes contradictory. Some of the stories about

Pheidias, one of the most celebrated ancient artists, exemplify this.

Pheidias, Plutarch tells us (*Life of Pericles* 13), was put in charge of all the public works constructed at the time of Pericles' ascendancy in Athens. Pericles was the statesman who guided the Athenian democracy at the peak of its political and creative power. The Parthenon and the Propylaea on the acropolis (6.5) were erected under his influence. Pheidias, his friend, as general overseer must have guided and supervised the execution of the architectural sculpture of the Parthenon (2.16–2.19, 2.21 and 7.6), though he did not do any work on it with his own hand. He was much too busy at the time creating the great *chryselephantine* (gold and ivory) statue of Athena that was to go inside the temple. Pheidias was most renowned for his huge chryselephantine statues of gods – he made another one, of Zeus, for Olympia – though he also worked in bronze and marble.

Because of his friendship with Pericles, we hear more of Pheidias than of most artists of the archaic and classical periods. Plutarch (*Life of Pericles* 31) recounts that political enemies of Pericles tried to attack the statesman through the artist he favoured. They accused Pheidias of having embezzled some of the gold intended for the statue of Athena, and when the charge was convincingly disproved, they accused him of impiously representing himself and Pericles on the shield of the statue, for which supposed indiscretion he was taken off to prison, where he died. Plutarch implies that these events took place shortly after the statue of Athena was completed, but archaeologists have established that Pheidias went to Olympia to make his Zeus *after* he had finished his work for the Parthenon. Since, furthermore, Pausanias (v.14.5) tells us that descendants of Pheidias continued to hold a special position at Olympia for many generations, the story that the great sculptor ended his life in an Athenian prison seems unlikely to be true.

We must, obviously, be cautious in our use of literary sources. If, however, we use them carefully, we can occasionally attach a name and a reputation to an original sculpture or a Roman copy. One can enjoy the art of Greece and Rome by just looking at it, but for an understanding of its history and development and of the context in which great works were created and the influence they exerted, the written sources are essential.

4 Sculpture

THE DECLINE OF THE CLASSICAL POLEIS AND THE RISE OF THE HELLENISTIC KINGDOMS

The Peloponnesian war took a heavy toll. Powerful Athens had been defeated, but mighty Sparta had also been weakened. For a little while in the fourth century BC, Thebes gained military ascendancy, but it was limited in time and influence. No force seemed able to unite or subjugate the Greek poleis permanently. By the end of the first century BC all this had changed. Dominated first by Macedonia and then by Rome, the poleis were never again to have anything more than nominal independence.

Though the Macedonians were a Greek-speaking people, they differed profoundly from the citizens of the Greek poleis. They were ruled by kings and lived more or less on the fringes of Greek civilization. Philip II, who ruled from about the middle of the fourth century BC, nevertheless appreciated what was best in Greek culture. He enticed to his court one of the most renowned Greek philosophers of the day – Aristotle – to act as tutor for his son and also, perhaps, one of the greatest Greek painters, whose name is lost to us, to decorate the royal tombs (5.2). Philip dreamed of leading the Greeks in an expedition against the Persians to avenge the Persian invasion of the early fifth century BC. Through keen political shrewdness and aptly deployed military might, he had by 338 BC conquered or made allies of all the Greek poleis on the mainland. But before he could turn his dream into reality, he was murdered.

His twenty-year-old son Alexander, known to later ages as 'the Great', succeeded to Philip's throne and to his plans. The recently subjugated Greek poleis took the first available opportunity to rebel against Macedonian domination. Alexander's response was swift and characteristic. To serve as an example he had the entire city of Thebes razed to the ground – except for the house owned in the previous century by the celebrated poet Pindar. The rebellion was quelled. Henceforth the Greeks, like the Macedonians, followed quietly where Alexander led, until his mighty armies had advanced right into India. Then the soldiers refused to go on. Alexander, obliged to turn back, died in Babylon in 323 BC at the age of 32. He had conquered all the lands from the Ionian Sea to the Punjab and from the Caucasus to the borders of Ethiopia. He left no adult heir.

Alexander's huge empire fell apart. His generals, able and gifted men, remained in control of several parts of the empire, but constantly at odds with one another. Their rivalries were inherited by their descendants along with the lands they ruled. The empire split into vast kingdoms: Egypt ruled by the family of the Ptolemies; western Asia by the Seleucids; Greece dominated and Macedonia ruled by the Antigonids. From the early third century BC to the later second, the enterprising and cultured dynasty of the Attalids carved out a domain for themselves in Asia Minor, centred on their capital at Pergamon. There were also some smaller kingdoms, and some venerable Greek cities were nominally free. In the meantime, little appreciated by anybody but the Attalids, the power of Rome was growing. By 31 BC the entire Hellenistic world had been absorbed into the Roman empire.

The kingdoms of the Hellenistic world were very different from the poleis of the Hellenic world. 'Hellenic' is an adjective that the Greeks in ancient times used to describe themselves. 'Hellenistic' is a modern adjective used to describe the period between the death of Alexander and the final conquest of the Greek-speaking world by Rome. It means 'resembling the original Hellenes' and is related to 'Hellenic' as 'realistic' is related to 'real'.

The Hellenistic kingdoms were ruled by Greco-Macedonian dynasties, the successors of Alexander. Cities on the Greek model had been founded along Alexander's path of conquest and settled by his Greek and Macedonian soldiers. These cities differed from those of the mother country both in size and in political structure; they were often vast metropoleis like Alexandria or Antioch, and they were not free in anything but name.

The intimacy and independence of the Hellenic polis were gone for ever. Men, being no longer citizens of a polis but rather subjects of huge kingdoms, felt they no longer belonged to a group, but only to themselves. Public buildings had dominated the old cities in

Greece and private houses had been extremely modest. Private houses in Hellenistic cities, by contrast, ranged from comfortable to luxurious, for they were the domain of the individual. Public monuments were also grand, but they were built by the monarchs, not the people. The temper of the times had radically changed.

The cities were dominated by Greeks – many new settlers had migrated to them from the homeland – but the surrounding peoples were quickly attracted to these centres of higher civilization. They tried to absorb Greek culture, but inevitably they broadened, distorted and vulgarized it.

The new tendencies that developed in Hellenistic art can already be discerned in the fourth century BC.

NEW TRENDS IN SCULPTURE IN THE FOURTH CENTURY BC

Three new trends distinguish sculpture in the fourth century BC from that of the second half of the fifth. First, there was a vigorous new push towards naturalism and with it a revival of interest in differentiation. Human beings were characterized not only in terms of age and personality, as they had been in the first half of the fifth century, but now also in terms of emotion and mood. Second, there was increasing specialization, even among artists, some of whom became adept in the rendering of passion and others in portraying more lyrical moods and gentler emotions. Third, new concepts – often even abstract ideas – became subjects for art. These could be conveyed by means of personifications, that is, representations in human form of concepts (like Peace), or states of mind (like Madness). Modern personifications such as the figure of Britannia on the old British penny or the Statue of Liberty in New York harbour are derived from this Greek tradition.

All three trends were exploited by the citizens of Megara, near Athens, when they commissioned five new statues for their temple of Aphrodite. They had an old ivory image of Aphrodite, the goddess of love, but towards the middle of the fourth century BC, they decided to amplify the meaning of the sanctuary in almost philosophical terms. The Megarians asked Skopas, a sculptor from the island of Paros who was distinguished for his representations of passion, to create statues representing Love, Desire, and Yearning, and Praxiteles, an Athenian noted for his rendering of the tenderer emotions, to sculpt the gentler figures of Persuasion and Consolation.

Thus the Megarians encouraged sculptors to produce images of emotions and moods hitherto little explored in the visual arts; they took advantage of the specialities of famous artists, and finally they made explicit five different aspects of the goddess Aphrodite. Giving concepts a visible and human form was an artistic response to contemporary philosophical thought which was engaged in clarifying similar analytic ideas.

In the first half of the fifth century (500–450 BC), Greek artists had tried to capture in stone or bronze the subtle qualities that distinguish men of different ages and temperaments. The sensitivity of these characterizations had given a breadth of humanity to Greek art that made it far outdistance anything that had been seen before. In the second half of the century (450–400 BC), however, there had been a shift of emphasis away from the exploration of diversity and towards the creation of a universal ideal. The impetus for this shift derived chiefly from the influence and prestige of the two greatest sculptors of the age: Pheidias, the director of works on the Parthenon, who was praised for his sublime portrayal of the gods, and Polykleitos, the Argive bronze-caster, who created unsurpassed images of men. Both had died by the early years of the fourth century BC, and with their passing there came a revival of interest in naturalism, diversity, and characterization. These tendencies, which gave the art of the fourth century its special character, continued to be explored and elaborated in the succeeding Hellenistic period.

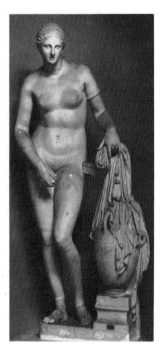

4.1 Knidian Aphrodite by Praxiteles, Roman copy of the original made *c.* 370 BC, height 204 cm, Vatican Museum, Rome.

THE FEMALE NUDE: A NEW SUBJECT IN ART

Praxiteles was renowned for statues that conveyed lyrical emotions. His most famous creation was a nude Aphrodite which was bought by the citizens of Knidos. The statue was extravagantly praised for its beauty, the melting glance of the eyes, the radiance and joyousness of the expression. Poems were written to celebrate it – in one, the goddess herself is supposed to have exclaimed 'Wherever did Praxiteles see me naked?' – men fell in love with it, and an enthusiastic collector, Nikomedes, the Hellenistic king of Bithynia, was so smitten by it that he offered to cancel the whole of the Knidian public debt (which was enormous) in exchange for it. But the Knidians wisely declined, for the statue made their city famous.

The statue is now lost. From uninspired Roman copies (4.1) it is difficult to see what all the fuss was about. The colouring of the original must have made a great difference, giving a soft blush to the cheeks and imparting a wonderful melting glance to the eyes. Praxiteles himself, when asked which of his statues he considered the finest, replied 'Those which Nikias has painted'. Nikias was also a famous painter of pictures, but he apparently did not feel that painting Praxiteles' statues was beneath his dignity.

Even through the clumsy Roman copy, one can grasp something of the beautiful ease and self-containment of the original pose. Praxiteles has cleverly applied the Polykleitan invention of contrapposto to the female form. Notice the contracted side of the body (to our left) where the hip rises and the shoulder drops. On the other side, the hip of the relaxed leg is lowered and the shoulder of the arm holding the drapery rises so that the line of the torso is extended. The inner harmony, the balance of a living organism, the sense of freedom and of repose which made Polykleitos' Spear-bearer a classic work (1.23–1.25) is just as effective here, but a new dimension has been gained by the application of Polykleitan principles to the rounded forms of the female nude: sensuousness.

This is easier to appreciate in a Renaissance drawing by Raphael (4.2). The contrapposto is the same, but more obvious and easier to see; the Praxitelean invention has been sensitively applied. Like the Roman copy, this drawing is not an original. The figure was created by Leonardo da Vinci but like Praxiteles' work it is lost, and Raphael's drawing is only a copy – a copy, however, by a great artist.

Though the male nude had long been accepted as a challenging subject for artists, Praxiteles was revolutionary when he created a major statue representing a nude female figure. She is shown with the naturalism to be expected in the fourth century BC, not only naturalism of form and detail, but also of action, for she holds her clothes quite simply, having just taken them off to prepare for a bath.

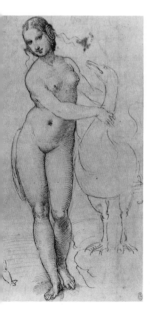

4.2 Raphael drawing, copy of 'Leda' by Leonardo da Vinci, showing the use of contrapposto, early 16th century, 30.8 × 19.2 cm, Windsor Castle.

The bath water is ready in the jar to her left (the combination of clothing and jar supplying the necessary support for the marble arm of the original). The inert fall of the drapery and the rigidity of the hydria contrast piquantly with the soft living forms of the body. The goddess holds her right hand in front of her genitals. This might be interpreted as a gesture of modesty, but it is more likely that, since this is an image of Aphrodite, the goddess is here indicating the source of her power, just as the bath she is about to take is a ritual bath, not just an everyday affair. The graceful integration of natural appearance and religious significance is one of the great achievements of Praxiteles.

If we try to imagine Praxiteles' statue of Aphrodite as it originally was, radiantly poised, gracious and beautiful, it is not difficult to understand that once a female nude had been portrayed in this expressive pose, the pose was copied, varied and developed throughout antiquity and from the time of the Renaissance rediscovery of antiquity up to modern times. Only in the fourth century BC did the female body come to be appreciated in art; its success thereafter became so great that eventually it almost eclipsed the male.

Besides the wholly nude Aphrodite, the fourth century BC also produced a half-draped type (4.3). We do not know the name of the artist who created the original statue of which the 'Aphrodite of Capua' is a Roman copy. It portrayed the goddess with her whole sensuous torso revealed, holding a shield to her left and in its reflection admiring her own beauty. The shield (now lost) kept the drapery of the legs in place to produce a work which, through hints and partial concealment, is as erotic as any nude. The invention was much appreciated and was copied, with variations, for centuries.

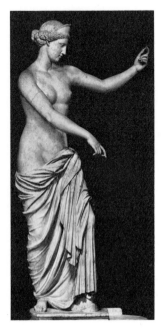

4.3   Aphrodite of Capua, Roman copy of an original of the mid 4th century BC, height 210 cm, Museo Nazionale, Naples.

NEW PROBLEMS IN THE HELLENISTIC PERIOD:
FIGURES IN SPACE

The Spear-bearer of Polykleitos (1.23–1.25) embodied the classic solution to the problem of presenting a figure in motion that was effective and handsome from all four principal views. By the beginning of the third century BC this solution was no longer

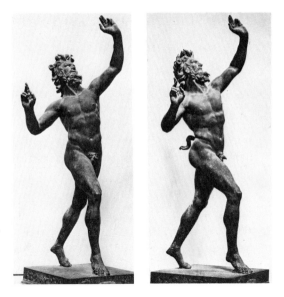

4.4 Two views of the dancing faun, Roman bronze copy of an original of the first half of the 3rd century BC, height 71 cm, Museo Nazionale, Naples.

4.5 Diagram showing the rotation of the body of the dancing faun (4.4).

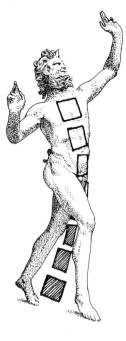

considered satisfactory – or rather, the problems it solved were no longer sufficiently stimulating. Sculptors, particularly those working in bronze, now wished to create figures that looked beautiful from *all* points of view, and which in fact led the eye (and the observer) round them. As if this were not difficult enough, the demands of the new naturalism insisted that the resulting pose should be rationally motivated, not just some arbitrary distortion for artistic purposes.

A work which satisfied all these conditions is the dancing faun that was found in Pompeii, a fine bronze statue that was probably an expensive Roman copy of a Greek original of the early third century BC (4.4). The joyous movement of the dance into which this half-wild creature whole-heartedly throws himself naturally produces a dramatically twisted pose. The diagram (4.5) shows what would happen if a rectangle of cardboard, white on one side and hatched on the other, were placed on the plane of the shoulders, the chest, the abdomen, and then progressively on the planes connecting the knees, the calves, and the feet; the consequent rotation of the cardboard along with the twist of the body is clearly apparent.

Two views are enough to show how satisfactory the design is as seen from different angles. At the same time, the figure looks perfectly natural. Not only is the movement natural, but also the anatomy – far more so than in works of the fifth century BC. Compare the head, with its clear delineation of windblown hair, bony structure, and soft pouches of skin, with the smooth head of

59

the Spear-bearer, or contrast the sinewy body with its careful distinctions of texture between the firm and the flaccid and between muscles, fat and bone with the body of the Spear-bearer, which consists entirely of suggestive generalizations lacking in such specific detail (1.23–1.25).

HELLENISTIC VARIETY:
NEW SUBJECTS – FOREIGNERS AND GROUPS

The search for new problems to solve was a constant stimulus to artists. By the middle of the third century BC, naturalistic representation had been fully mastered and could be effectively combined with a multiplicity of viewpoints in single figures. It was a challenge to try to do the same thing with a free-standing group.

The Greeks had considerable experience in working with groups of figures when they designed pediments (2.9–2.12), but these were seen only from the front. A free-standing group, visible from all sides, was quite another matter. Such groups became very popular in the third and second centuries BC and were often powerfully expressive as well as aesthetically satisfying.

A group showing a Gaul who has just killed his wife and is about to kill himself must have been magnificent in the original. The Roman copy (4.6), even with its faulty restoration (the extended arm of the wife should hang parallel to her other arm) is still impressive. The group is roughly pyramidal. It is complex, interesting and revealing from all sides. But there is more than just artistic skill and formal achievement here; there is also a sense of drama and pathos.

The work was set up in Pergamon, a Hellenistic city in Asia Minor (now Turkey), as the centrepiece of a war memorial. The Pergamenes had recently repulsed an incursion of the Gauls and were justifiably proud of their victory. They felt they had done as much to preserve Hellenistic civilization in the face of a barbarian invasion as the Athenians had in the fifth century BC when they defeated the Persians.

The Pergamenes' sense of triumph did not lead them to belittle the heroic enemy they had beaten. In fact, respect for the enemy was an old part of the Greek tradition. Even as far back as the Homeric

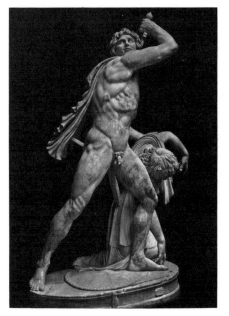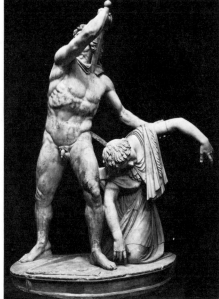

4.6 Two views of the Gaul killing his wife and himself, Roman copy of an original of the second half of the 3rd century BC, height 211 cm, Museo Nazionale delle Terme, Rome.

epics, the Trojan Hector is portrayed as valiant and brave. Similarly here the Gauls are depicted in full dignity. The noble adversary, who sees that defeat is inevitable, is too proud to submit. Only death will conquer him. He has killed his wife because he loves her. In the *Iliad*, Hector laments for his wife, foreseeing that when Troy falls she will become a slave. The Gaul will not permit this fate to overtake *his* wife. As she falls limply to the ground, he looks back, defiant to the last, and prepares to plunge the sword into his throat.

The contrasts implicit in the scene – living and dead, man and woman, draped and nude – are all dramatically accentuated. Notice how the lifeless feminine arm of the wife hangs beside the strong, tense, masculine leg of her husband.

The Gauls, who were tall with thick hair and hard muscles, were physically very different from the Mediterranean types with whom they fought. Hellenistic artists revelled in portraying the differences. The scope of art had by now greatly widened. Nude women, barbarians, children, old people – all were now considered challenges to artists and worthy of portrayal. This was part of the more tolerant and less exclusive attitude that pervaded Hellenistic society. The interest in naturalism combined with the interest in foreign types led to some of the most sensitive depictions of Gauls, African negroes, and South Russian Scythians that have ever been produced.

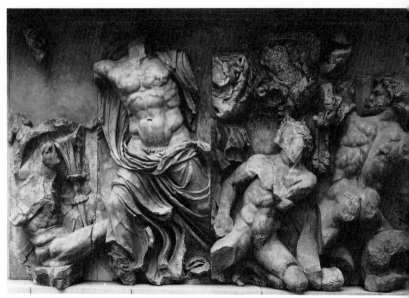

4.7 The central part of the west side of the Pergamon altar showing Zeus and Athena fighting giants, first half of the 2nd century BC (*c.* 180–160 BC), height 230 cm, Staatliche Museen, E. Berlin.

NEW DRAMA IN OLD COMPOSITIONS

The group of the Gaul and his wife was erected in the second half of the third century BC, shortly after a Pergamene defeat of the invading Gauls. Half a century later, probably between 180 and 160 BC, a still more elaborate monument was set up in Pergamon. It took the form of a huge altar to the chief of the gods, Zeus, the base of which was decorated with a dramatic portrayal of the battle of the gods and giants (4.7).

The relief is extremely high and the figures almost burst out of the background. Bulging muscles and swirling drapery convey a tremendous sense of explosive energy. The centrepiece on the west side, the first a visitor would encounter, showed Zeus (to the left), his powerful body revealed as his drapery slips from his shoulder, simultaneously fighting three giants, while Athena (to the right) turns back to dispose of another. The giants, who are getting the worst of it, are shown with snake legs, or winged, or in ordinary human form. One falls to the left of Zeus and is shown in profile; another, smitten, collapses on his knees to the right, his body in a three-quarter view reflecting the three-quarter view of Zeus; a third (further right) rises on his snake legs to fight on and is shown in back view. This careful arrangement and variation of the positions of the figures is not immediately obvious, but it contributes to the effect of the whole. Actually, the arrangement is based on a fifth-century-BC

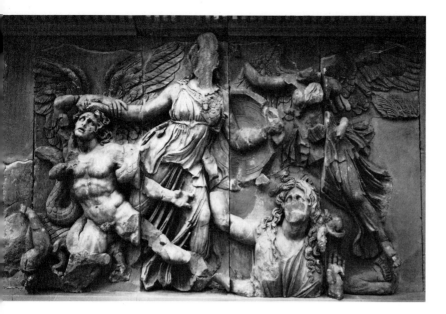

Athenian relief and is not the only classical reminiscence in the work, as we shall see.

Athena, striding vigorously away from Zeus, seizes her adversary by the hair (4.7). His wings fill the upper part of the relief. He looks up at her with anguished eyes – this is a further development of that expression of pathos and drama for which Skopas was famous in the fourth century BC (p. 55). To the right of Athena the goddess Earth, mother of the giants, rises up from her own element and with painfully drawn brows begs Athena to spare the life of her son. Athena is unmoved, and a winged Victory, knowing the outcome, flies over Earth's head to crown Athena.

The dominant motif of Zeus and Athena, powerful god and goddess, moving in opposite directions but turning back to look at each other, is the very composition (though reversed) used in the west pediment of the Parthenon (2.12). This visual quotation would have been obvious to any observer in antiquity and would have underlined the claim of the Pergamene kings to be the cultural heirs of the fifth-century Athenians. It is a splendid and creative adaptation of a great work of the past.

USES AND ABUSES OF THE PAST

In time, adaptations of works of the past became less creative, as if

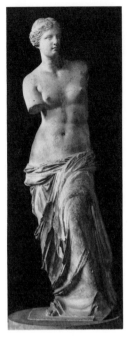

4.8 Aphrodite from
Melos ('Venus de Milo'),
second half of the 2nd
century BC, height
204 cm, Louvre, Paris.

some of the fire had gone out of Greek artists. A characteristic work
of the second half of the second century (150–100 BC) is the
celebrated Aphrodite of Melos ('Venus de Milo') (4.8). A half-
draped figure of the goddess, she obviously combines the partial
nudity and the pose of the Aphrodite of Capua (4.3) with the
contrapposto and facial type of Praxiteles' Knidian Aphrodite (4.1).
The amalgam is successful, and the statue is justly famous, but it is
much more obviously derivative than the Zeus and Athena on the
Pergamon altar.

The dependence of artists on the past grew heavier with time.
Imitations of older works became less creative. An example from the
first century BC illustrates this sorry degeneration (4.9). Two figures
are combined to produce the group of Orestes and Electra,
mythological brother and sister. Orestes is modelled on an early
fifth-century-BC type of youth, and Electra is practically a copy of
the late fifth-century-BC 'Venus Genetrix' (1.29) with only slight
variations – for instance the right arm moved to rest across the
youth's shoulders and the drapery adjusted for greater modesty. It is
a dry work, an unattractive pasting together of two unrelated older
statues that makes the Aphrodite of Melos (4.8) look fresh and
original by comparison.

The group is not worked out in terms of space and depth; the two
figures are just strung out along a single plane. Front and back views
would be satisfactory, but the side views are virtually worthless.
There was now a vogue, which continued under the Romans, for
displaying statues against a wall, so that many groups (and even
single figures) were designed for one view only.

It is but a short step from unimaginative adaptations like the
Orestes and Electra group (4.9) to the production of exact copies of
older masterpieces. This had begun by the later first century BC and
was greatly stimulated by demand from the Romans. The Romans
then ruled Greece, but had come under the sway of Greek art. They
needed copies for decoration and display. The production of copies
began at this time to play a significant role in the economics and
technique of Greek sculpture; the Romans, as patrons, now called
the tune.

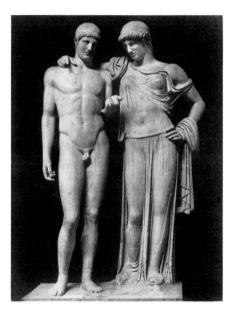

4.9 Orestes and Electra, 1st century BC, height 139 cm, Museo Nazionale, Naples.

THE HELLENISTIC CONTRIBUTION

A great deal of sculpture was made during the Hellenistic period; we have touched on only a few characteristic examples. The most significant trends were a widening of subject matter (to include female nudes as well as male, foreigners as well as Greeks, extremes of babyhood and old age as well as the ideal of youthful maturity); a deepening of emotional characterizations (with special emphasis on the portrayal of suffering and pain, dramatically conveyed through facial expression, turbulent drapery, and expressive pose of the body); and formal innovations (including the invention of the many-sided, twisting figure and complex free-standing groups).

Individual sculptors travelled widely during the Hellenistic period and worked more for private patrons than for the political communities or sanctuaries of the gods they had served in the past. The taste and preferences of individual patrons increasingly directed the development of sculptural style.

By the middle of the second century BC admiration for the art of the past began to influence the design of sculptures, at first through creative adaptations and visual allusions, but eventually through increasingly lifeless imitations. Exact copies, which began to be made with mechanical aids at the very end of the Hellenistic period, though totally lacking in creative input, nevertheless come as an improvement by contrast with the poor stuff that had preceded them.

5 Painting

Although we know that many masterpieces were painted in the fourth century BC and the Hellenistic period, hardly anything has survived. In order to get some idea of what painting was like at that time we have to rely on three sources of information: pictures on pottery, copies of paintings made for the Romans, and descriptions by ancient authors. None of these is entirely satisfactory.

Vase painters never copied wall paintings exactly, but they sometimes made use of new ideas about the treatment of space, perspective and the handling of light that are so alien to the technique of vase painting that we can deduce that they must have been inspired by developments in free painting. After the fifth century BC, vase painting became a minor art and could only dimly reflect the great achievements taking place elsewhere.

Copies of Greek paintings made for the Romans, though closer to the sources of their inspiration than paintings on pottery, are not so accurate as the more mechanically produced Roman copies of statues. Sometimes, when we can compare several copies of the same original, it becomes obvious that the Roman painters freely adapted, changed and modified their models (8.1 and 8.2).

Descriptions by ancient writers, though often vivid and entertaining, can never bring lost works before our eyes. They have stimulated artists from the time of the Renaissance on, who have produced splendid and original works in an effort to re-create Greek paintings, but these works tell us only about the painters who made them, not the paintings the ancient author saw.

THE FOURTH CENTURY BC AND ITS LEGACY

It is a great pity we have so little evidence about the painting of the fourth century BC, for it was clearly full of exciting novelty and invention. The painters, Pliny tells us, were lively personalities and great technical innovators.

By the end of the fourth century BC, foreshortening of the body (human and horse) had been brought to perfection; modelling in terms of light and shadow had been mastered; the effects of highlights and even reflected lights had been studied; the expression of emotion had been explored; and some rudimentary work on perspective had been done.

A summary of the achievements of the painters of the fourth century BC can be seen in a Roman mosaic that is a copy of a painting probably made at the beginning of the third century BC (5.1). A mosaic is made up mostly of tiny squares of stones of different colours assembled to make a pattern or look like a picture. The Greeks had become technically accomplished in the making of mosaics in the course of the third century BC. When this mosaic was made for a Pompeian client in the first century BC, mosaicists were able to use such minute pieces of stone and such a wide range of colours that they were able to reproduce even very elaborate and subtle paintings. This example, known as the Alexander mosaic, is such a copy. The painting glorified and dramatized Alexander the Great's victory over the Persian king Darius III.

Although parts of the mosaic have been destroyed, we can still see how vividly a sense of the mêlée of battle has been conveyed, while at the same time the chief characters in this historical drama have been kept prominent.

Alexander, helmetless, his hair blowing in the wind, rides forward energetically from the left. His head is clearly silhouetted against the sky. He has thrust his spear through one of Darius' devoted servants, who was just clambering off his fallen horse when Alexander's spear pierced his side. To his right, another Persian nobleman has dismounted and holds the head of his restive horse. This chestnut horse is seen from the rear, superbly foreshortened, with effective highlights glancing off its rump and rather more tentative shadows cast by its legs. Meanwhile, Darius looks back from his chariot and reaches out a compassionate hand towards the follower who is ready to die for him – a portrayal showing characteristic Greek respect for the enemy. Darius' head and his

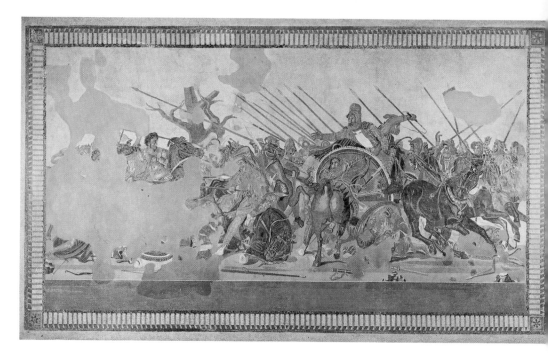

5.1 Alexander mosaic showing the battle of Alexander the Great and Darius III, Roman copy of an original of the early 3rd century BC, height 217 cm, Museo Nazionale, Naples.

helpless extended arm are silhouetted against the sky. He is the counterpart of Alexander; the two kings oppose each other above the heads of all the other figures. But there is not a moment's doubt who the victor will be.

Darius' charioteer, slightly to the right of the king, furiously whips the horses on to make a greater effort, careless that they may run down the fallen warrior whose back is to us, but whose face is reflected in his polished shield. The black horses of Darius' chariot gallop forward and to the right: once again the skilful use of highlights and foreshortening makes the complex arrangement clear.

It is amazing that such subtlety of modelling and such evocative colour gradations can be caught in the relatively crude mosaic technique. The colour range is restrained – there are no greens or blues – but this was probably a characteristic of the original painting, not its translation into mosaic, for Pliny tells us that some painters restricted their palette to just four colours – red, yellow, black and white (and, of course, mixtures of these).

While the technical achievements of the painters up to the end of the fourth century BC are splendidly revealed by this mosaic, so are their limitations. The whole drama is acted out on a narrow stage, the depth of which is defined only by the foreshortening of the

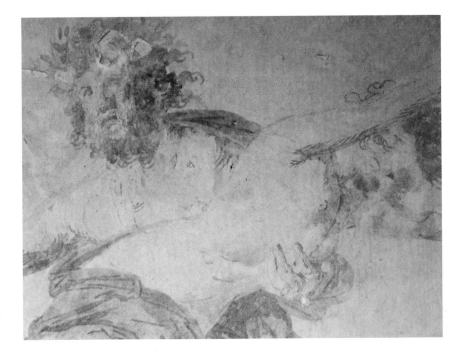

5.2 Painting from the Macedonian royal tombs showing Pluto abducting Persephone, second half of the 4th century BC, Vergina, Greece.

figures and their overlappings. The setting, too, has received short shrift. A few rocks on the ground and a single dead tree do for a landscape.

The Alexander mosaic is very imposing. The creation of a great artist has been transmitted, with only slight loss of effect, through the skill of the mosaic copyist. Nevertheless it does not have the stunning impact of a direct encounter with an outstanding work of art.

In contrast, the paintings discovered in 1977 that decorated the royal tombs at Vergina in Macedonia – though much damaged – are truly staggering. One scene that is better preserved than most shows the god of the Underworld, Pluto, abducting the corn maiden Persephone. The girl was picking flowers with her friends when the god emerged from the earth, seized her, and carried her off in his chariot. A detail (5.2) shows the urgent god, his hair blowing wildly as he grasps the tender body of the girl, only one of whose frightened eyes is now visible. The freedom and power of the brush-strokes, the certainty of effects, the intensity of emotion – all reveal the hand of a truly great artist, one having the calibre of a Rubens or a Raphael. Such stature is seldom apparent in the paintings that have come down to us from antiquity.

HELLENISTIC ACHIEVEMENTS: NEW THEMES AND SETTINGS

The paintings on the royal tombs at Vergina give us a glimpse of the quality of the work that must have been produced by the greatest Greek painters of the fourth century BC. But it is a solitary glimpse. In order to learn more about how Hellenistic painting developed we must rely primarily on literary sources and the evidence from Roman copies.

The Hellenistic period was one of great expansion for the Greeks, not only geographically but also artistically and intellectually. Painting, like sculpture, showed not only considerable technical advances, but also a widening of themes. Before the Hellenistic period paintings had dealt chiefly with mythological subjects and occasionally, as in the Alexander mosaic, with historical scenes. Now with artists' greater interest in ordinary people, their everyday life and everyday things, the range of subjects considered appropriate for painting broadened.

Pliny says that a certain Peiraikos painted barbers' shops, cobblers' stalls, asses, eatables and similar subjects, earning for himself the name of 'painter of odds and ends'. Such a selection of themes, quite lacking in moral uplift, would hardly have appealed to Polygnotos, but it did, by the third century BC, present an exciting challenge to many painters. An echo of the kind of excerpt of daily life that Peiraikos favoured can perhaps be seen in a fine mosaic which is a copy of a third-century-BC painting (5.3). It shows a commonplace scene: a group of street musicians (all of whom are wearing masks) and a poor boy, who either accompanies them or is just an onlooker. The modelling of the figures is fully convincing and the play of light is handled with consummate skill. Notice the accurate rendering of the cast shadow of the tambourine player as it falls on the pavement and then climbs up the wall, and the bright highlights and deep shadows in the shiny clothes of the musicians. The space above the players and to the side is generous, but depth is still restricted to a narrow shelf on which the action takes place.

The broadening of subject matter meant that flora and fauna became themes for paintings as well as men and gods; Hellenistic artists created many still-lifes and animal paintings. Let us consider just one example.

The most famous mosaicist in antiquity was Sosos, who lived in Pergamon in the second century BC. Among his celebrated works was one that represented doves drinking. A Roman copy of this work (appropriately, in mosaic) (5.4) gives some hint of the serenity of the subject and the dignity that can be imparted even to birds. The copy, nevertheless, lacks one feature that was particularly praised in the original: the shadow in the water of the dove that has its head inclined into the bowl to drink. A subtle effect indeed this must have been!

Probably around the middle of the second century BC, artists became seriously interested in the representation of space in its own right, not just as the ambience in which people and things exist. Painted scenery for tragedies had already in the fifth century BC stimulated an interest in perspective. The painter Agatharchos is supposed to have painted a perspective setting for a play by Aeschylus (probably a revival) and to have inspired contemporary scientists to undertake a theoretical study of the subject (p.50). One rather suspects (from looking at vase paintings of the fourth century BC) that the system of perspective was still rather haphazard, but by the first century BC, when Roman painters copied and adapted Greek perspective settings (5.5), much progress had been made.

There was a vogue for painting architectural vistas in Rome during the first century BC (8.4). Since these vistas, whether they represent cities, palaces, or sanctuaries, contain no human figures, we may assume that they were inspired by stage sets, which in the theatre would have been peopled by actors.

A cityscape found at Boscoreale near Pompeii provides a charming example (5.5). A firmly shut door within a wall defines the front plane of this architectural painting. Above the wall one catches delightful glimpses of the city – a balcony jutting out to the right, an enclosed tower rising to the left, two houses between, with a ladder reaching to an upstairs window. In the distance, long colonnades stretch off to the right. Skilfully applied shadows within the wide tonal range of warm reds, glowing yellows, clear whites and tranquil blues help to convey a sense of depth and distance, but it is the receding lines of the buildings themselves that do most to suggest space. The perspective, however, is neither unified nor consistent. Each element is foreshortened more or less independently without

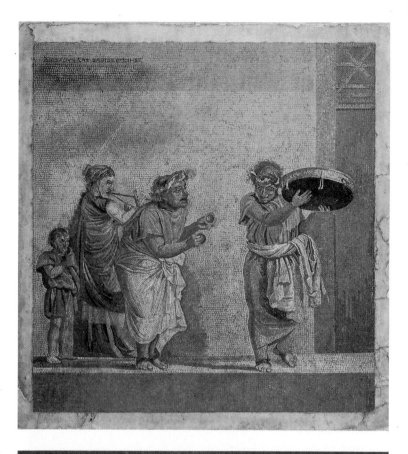

5.3 Mosaic showing
street musicians, Roman
copy of an original of the
3rd century BC, height
43.7 cm, Museo
Nazionale, Naples.

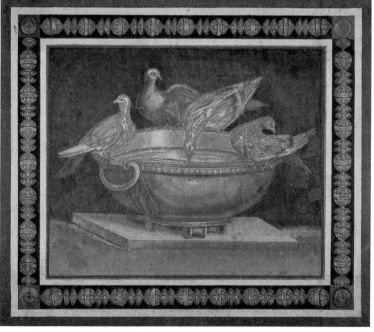

5.4 Mosaic showing
doves drinking, Roman
copy probably of an
original by Sosos of
Pergamon made in the
2nd century BC, height
85 cm, Museo
Capitolino, Rome.

5.5 Wall painting from Boscoreale showing a city, Roman copy of a Greek painting of the 2nd century BC, height 244 cm, Metropolitan Museum of Art, New York, Rogers Fund, 1903.

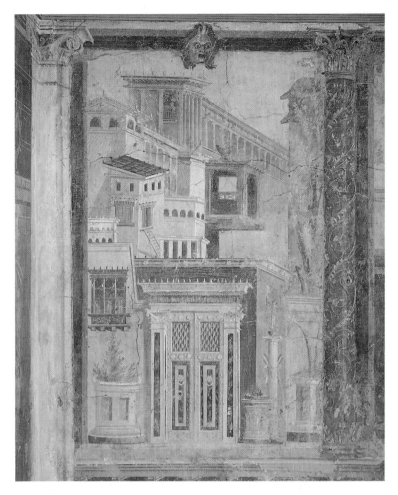

below

5.6 Wall painting, one of a series showing scenes from the *Odyssey*: Odysseus in the Underworld, Roman copy of a Greek painting of the 2nd or 1st century BC, height preserved 150 cm, Vatican Museum, Rome.

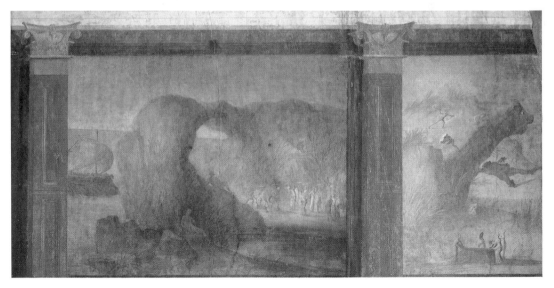

any regard to the whole. Such a piecemeal perspective scheme suggests that however evocative the Greeks made their architectural vistas, they never fully developed a single-point perspective system such as was later formulated in the Renaissance. This is the opinion of many scholars, but others disagree. They cite Roman architectural paintings in which no fewer than forty *orthogonals* (receding lines) meet at a single point, and argue that this could hardly have happened by chance. They believe that the Greeks had in fact mastered single-point perspective, but that the Roman copyists did not always transmit their achievements accurately.

While depth in architecture can be indicated by means of receding lines, depth in landscape can be suggested only by means of subtle changes in colour with distance and the blurring of the farthest features. This is exactly what we see in the so-called 'Odyssey landscapes' (5.6). These are Roman copies of late Hellenistic originals that illustrate episodes from the *Odyssey*, but they are very different from the seventh-century-BC krater showing a scene from the *Odyssey* (3.5) in which the figures are everything. In the Odyssey landscapes, by contrast, the figures are virtually lost in the breadth of the view. Odysseus' ship rides at anchor to the left, while the hero himself strides with a few friends through the eerie cavern that is the opening to the Underworld. The shadowy dead – small, wispy figures – emerge into the strange light to meet him. In the foreground, a river god (compare 2.20 and 2.21) reclines beside his element. But it is the landscape itself – rocks, caverns, sea and sky – all finally mastered by the painter's brush – that dominates the scene.

Painting was now as versatile as sculpture, as fully in command of all the resources of the medium. Hellenistic painters had learned how to represent space and light and they had introduced new subjects. Still-lifes, landscape, portraiture, genre painting – anything from lofty allegories to homely objects – all could now be rendered in paint. It was this richness in the range of themes and mastery of technique that the Greeks bequeathed to the Romans.

6 Architecture and planning

Several of the most important tendencies in the development of Hellenistic architecture can be grasped if we look at just three types of building: houses, theatres and sanctuaries.

THE HOUSE: NEW LUXURY IN PRIVATE LIFE

During the Hellenistic period, when people lived as part of huge kingdoms governed by remote rulers, they could no longer identify so immediately with their communities and began to feel isolated and alone. Their interest became focused on themselves, as emphasis, both emotional and economic, withdrew from the group and shifted on to the individual. People thought increasingly about their private lives and tried to make the intimate world around them more attractive and agreeable. They began to build more elaborate and comfortable houses for themselves; rulers, too, touched by the same sense of isolation, began to build palaces.

Fifth-century-BC houses in Athens had been very modest (6.1a). They usually consisted of two storeys and were built of unbaked brick on a low stone base. The entrance was somewhere along one side and led, sometimes rather indirectly, to a central courtyard. The courtyard was a simple affair, a source of light and air for the rooms that opened off it. A blank wall faced the street, pierced only by small windows whose height above the street ensured privacy.

By the fourth century BC such humble dwellings had, whenever possible, been improved upon. A contemporary orator noticed the distinctions that were then appearing between the rich and the poor and lamented the passing of the good old days when only public buildings caught the eye with their magnificence.

Houses built in the fourth century BC in Priene (a city on the west coast of Asia Minor) (6.1b) were squared up instead of being irregular, and fitted neatly into the newly laid out rectangular street

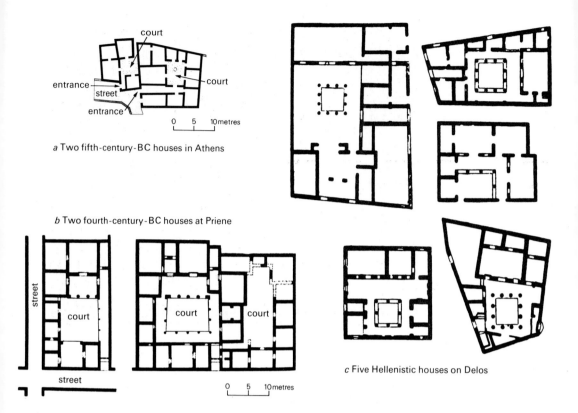

a Two fifth-century-BC houses in Athens

b Two fourth-century-BC houses at Priene

c Five Hellenistic houses on Delos

6.1 Plans of Greek houses from the 5th to 2nd centuries BC.

grid. Most rooms still opened off an inner courtyard, but this had become grander and sometimes had a row of columns along one side or even around all four sides (an internal peristyle).

By the Hellenistic period (6.1c) the courtyards of most houses were adorned with gracious peristyles. Many walls were now decorated to simulate marble inlays, and handsome mosaics were laid on the floors; this was the period in which Sosos worked (5.4). Notice how varied the designs of houses built in Delos in the Hellenistic period were (6.1c). The arrangement of the rooms, their size and relationship, and even the placement of the entrance are left to the individual. This freedom and lack of regimentation is characteristically Greek.

THE THEATRE: THE ACTOR BECOMES THE PRINCIPAL

The interest in the individual that led to the development of the spacious, attractive peristyle house also manifested itself in the development of the theatre. In drama as in life, emphasis came to be

76

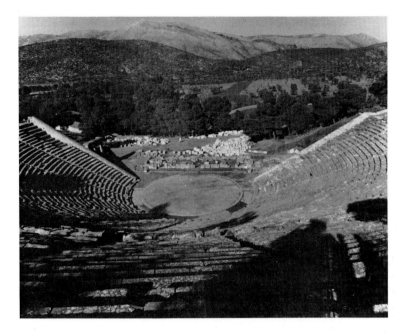

6.2 The theatre at Epidauros, 4th century BC.

placed ever more on the individual rather than the group; in drama, this meant the actor rather than the chorus.

Greek plays were performed as part of the celebrations in honour of the god Dionysus. In the earliest plays most of the action was provided by the chorus and the role of the individual actors was very limited. During the course of the fifth century BC, the actors became increasingly important, and by the time of the latest surviving comedy by Aristophanes, written in the first quarter of the fourth century BC (388), the chorus had virtually disappeared. It took a little while for staging and architecture to catch up with these developments.

In the fifth and fourth centuries BC, theatres had been designed with primary emphasis on the *orchestra*, the circular dancing place where the chorus performed and interacted with the actors. The *cavea* (*theatron*), carved out of the side of a hill, had grown as a watching place around the orchestra, a sort of natural grandstand that eventually was given an architectural form.

The beautiful fourth-century-BC theatre at Epidauros (6.2) gives a good idea what a classical theatre looked like. It consists of three visually independent parts: the round orchestra in the centre, the stage buildings on one side, and on the other the cavea, consisting of tier upon tier of seats sweeping round in something over a semicircle.

77

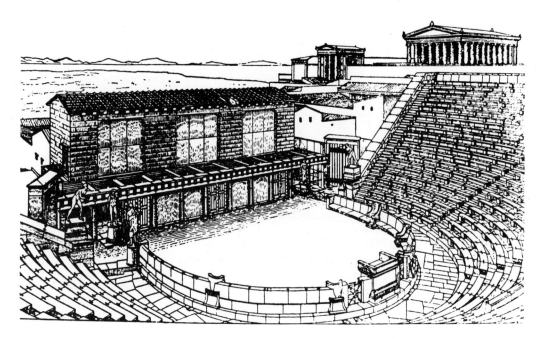

6.3 Drawing of the
3rd-century BC
renovation of the theatre
at Priene.

A splendid view of the countryside is to be had from the seats in
the theatre. Since Greek dramas were always performed in daylight,
this must have presented quite a challenge to playwrights, who had
to make their plays gripping enough to prevent the audience's
attention from wandering off into the landscape.

As actors became more and more important for the action and the
chorus dropped out, theatres were redesigned to accommodate the
new style of performance better. In the fifth- and fourth-century
theatres, the stage building had been used for storing props and sets.
In front of it there might be a single-storied façade, the *proskenion*,
against which the stage sets were placed. The roof of the proskenion
could be used occasionally for the appearance of gods, when such
was required by the play. Otherwise, all the action took place in the
orchestra.

By the second century BC, the theatre at Priene had been
remodelled (6.3) so that the actors could be isolated and elevated and
thus accorded the prominence that their parts demanded. This was
done by turning the roof of the proskenion into a stage. Great
openings were cut into the wall of the stage building behind the roof
of the proskenion. Stage sets and backdrops could be placed in these
gaps. The illusion of space that could eventually be conveyed by
such painted sets is suggested by the Roman paintings they inspired
(5.5). The orchestra and its backdrop now became less important

78

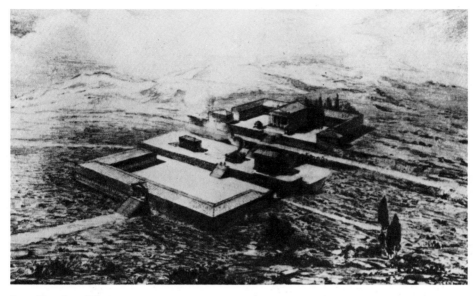

6.4 Drawing of the
sanctuary of Asclepius
on Kos, built from the
4th to the 2nd
centuries BC.

and the elevation of the actors on to a high stage brings us closer to
modern theatre practice.

When the proskenion roof became the acting stage, the proskenion itself was moved forward at the expense of the orchestra,
which now ceased to be a full circle (6.3). As a consequence, instead
of consisting of three fully independent parts, the theatre begins to
look more unified: cavea bonded to orchestra, orchestra attached to
the scene building. These tendencies were carried even further by
the Romans (9.8 and 9.9).

THE SANCTUARY: UNIFICATION OF COMPLEXES

As theatre design developed, architects became less interested in
preserving the independence of each individual part and more
inclined to bring the parts together. So, too, architects working on
larger complexes tried to unify spaces and relate buildings to one
another. A single example will clarify the principle, which applies no
less to city planning and civic centres than to sanctuaries.

The sanctuary of the god Asclepius on the island of Kos was built
over two centuries (from about 360 to 160 BC) and on three different
levels, yet the whole complex emerges as a unit (6.4). The 'U'-
shaped colonnaded *stoas* at the top and the bottom bind the elements
together, while the central flights of steps give a sense of unity,
ascent and climax.

79

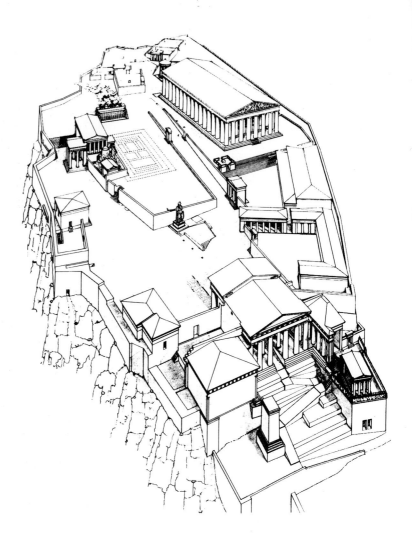

6.5 Drawing of the acropolis at Athens showing the placement of the major 5th-century BC buildings.

The impression is very different from that given by the layout of the temples and shrines on the Athenian acropolis (6.5). These were all built within a single half-century (448–406 BC), yet each building seems to have been thought out separately and there appears to have been little effort to organize the space as a whole. The large complex of structures towards the bottom of the drawing is the Propylaea, the entrance gate to the acropolis and its attached buildings. It has the same orientation as the Parthenon, the large temple to the upper right, but there is no axial connection between the two. Emerging from the Propylaea, one does not see the Parthenon from the front, but from one corner. On the opposite side of the acropolis (to the left of the drawing) is the small and elaborate Erechtheum, which contrasts markedly with the severe grandeur of the Parthenon.

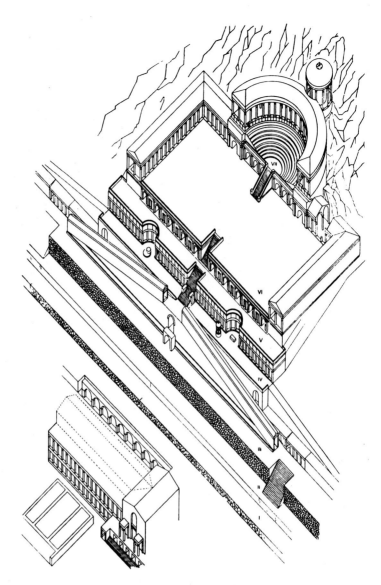

6.6 Drawing of the sanctuary of Fortuna at Praeneste, Roman, 1st century BC.

Other smaller buildings, offerings, and shrines are scattered freely about the precinct.

Although the impression of the sanctuary of Asclepius on Kos (6.4) is one of unity and balance, many of the parts have retained their independence and much of the symmetry is more apparent than real. Notice, for instance, the way the altar on the middle terrace is 'balanced' by a small temple. Nevertheless the design and placement of the individual elements is controlled by a sense for organizational coherence that was far less pronounced when the classical acropolis was built (6.5); but there was still a long way to go before architects could create the splendid order that the Romans imposed on an entire hillside at Praeneste in the first century BC (6.6).

The arrangement at Praeneste is strictly symmetrical. A strongly accentuated axis leads the eye straight up the centre of the complex. The small paired hemicycles on terrace IV herald the grand theatre-like hemicycle that crowns the sanctuary. Rigorous axial symmetry is combined with a most imaginative play of curved and rectangular forms to produce a climactic ascent to the apex. By contrast with this wonderful Roman discipline, the sanctuary at Kos preserves that touch of independence and freedom that is so characteristic of Greek art.

7 · Roman statues and reliefs

THE EMERGENCE OF THE ROMAN EMPIRE

We have already met the Romans several times in this book. We know they were great admirers of Greek art and ordered copies of sculptures and paintings which, in some cases, give us the only information we have about celebrated Greek originals (1.18, 1.23, 1.28 and 1.29; 4.1, 4.3, 4.4 and 4.6; 5.1, 5.3, 5.4, 5.5, and 5.6; and 8.1 and 8.2).

The city of Rome had begun in a small way in the eighth century BC. By the fourth century BC it had already established a republican form of government and begun that inexorable growth that was eventually to make it the centre of a vast empire.

Encounters with the Greeks began in earnest in the third century BC in south Italy and Sicily, where the Greeks had long established colonies. Roman admiration for the Greeks was soon tempered by irritation as rival Hellenistic powers began to call on Rome to assist them in their struggles, for the Hellenistic kings were as constantly at war with one another as the classical poleis had been. The Romans were militarily better organized than the Greeks and politically more efficient. When their patience ran out with the endlessly squabbling Greeks, they began to subjugate the Hellenistic kingdoms one by one. The last to fall was Egypt, conquered by Augustus in 31 BC. At the same time the republic vanished, leaving behind only a handful of traditional forms. Augustus, having finally eliminated all his rivals, became emperor and the Roman republic, though Augustus claimed to have restored it in 27 BC, became the Roman empire.

The huge empire flourished for well over two centuries, bringing peace and prosperity along with its domination, but it fell upon hard times during the third century AD. In 285 the emperor Diocletian stemmed the decline by astutely dividing the empire into four parts;

in 330 the emperor Constantine moved the imperial residence to Constantinople. Rome's days of grandeur were over.

Though the Romans dominated the Greeks politically and militarily, they submitted to their superiority in art and culture. The Roman poet Horace put it succinctly: 'Captive Greece led her rude captor captive.'

The Romans were fascinated not only with Greek art but also with Greek poetry, rhetoric, and philosophy. This was a great boon to Greek intellectuals and craftsmen – teachers, scholars, thinkers, sculptors and painters – for it was the enthusiastic Romans who gave them employment.

An immense amount of sculpture was carved during the period of the Roman empire (31 BC–AD 330); most of it consisted of copies of Greek statues. This provided business for the many hundreds of skilled sculptors throughout the empire who knew their materials and how to work them. These craftsmen were available, trained and ready when, occasionally, the Romans asked them to produce original works.

PORTRAITURE: SPECIFICITY OF PERSON

By temperament and by tradition the Romans were very different from the Greeks. While the Greeks enjoyed abstraction and generalization in thought and art, the Romans, down-to-earth and practical as they were, preferred the specific and the factual.

Greek portraits were almost exclusively of famous men and women: people who had won their reputation as athletes, poets, philosophers, rulers and orators. Something typical always clung to their representations to help define in what category they had won their fame. Roman portraits could be of anybody who had the means, family connections or distinction to commission them. What the Romans wanted from a portrait was the accurate image of a particular person. Under the influence of Greek art, sculptors working for the Romans often modified their style of portraiture and made their subjects look more beautiful or more powerful than they really were, but they did not sacrifice their unique characteristics, that specificity so highly valued by the Romans.

An impressive portrait of the first emperor, Augustus (31 BC–AD 14) (7.1), illustrates the sort of compromise that a Greek sculptor working to the order of a Roman patron could achieve.

Polykleitos' Spear-bearer (1.23) was the acme of classical sculpture, and the Romans deeply appreciated the air of serenity and dignity conferred on the figure by the carefully constructed pose. It was therefore chosen to provide the framework for a representation of Augustus that was meant to convey to his subjects both respect for his authority and admiration for his grace and control. But the Greek statue could hardly be taken over as a model just as it was, since it had several features that offended Roman taste.

First of all, the Spear-bearer was an ideal figure – perhaps a representation of the Homeric hero Achilles, but certainly not any real person. This had to be changed, and so the head of the Spear-bearer was modified as much as was necessary to capture the actual features of Augustus, which were, nevertheless made just beautiful enough to reflect the Spear-bearer's purity of form.

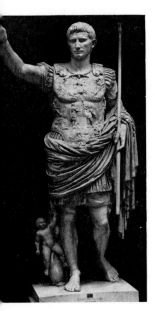

7.1 Augustus from Prima Porta, *c.* 19 BC, height 204 cm, Vatican Museum, Rome

Second, the Spear-bearer was nude. This was, of course, natural for a heroic Greek statue and furthermore essential to reveal the harmonious contrapposto. But it might have seemed improper for a Roman, especially for a Roman who posed as the guardian of ancient traditions of propriety and sobriety, as Augustus did. So the sculptor dressed his imperial subject in a suit of armour, and even gave him a cloak. The armour was, however, made so form-fitting that while decency was preserved, the modelling of the torso still remained clearly visible.

Third, the Spear-bearer lacked focus and direction. It was not felt right that the Roman emperor should stroll so dreamily through space. Rather, he should address his subjects directly and dominate the spectators who stood before him. Only slight modifications of the pose of the Spear-bearer were needed to bring this about: the head lifted and turned a little to look forward and outward, and the right arm raised to a commanding position. Thus Augustus, by gaze and by gesture, as if through the force of his personality, controls the space in front of him.

The statue was placed against a wall, as was often the case with Roman sculpture, and so all the emphasis is concentrated on the front view. The sides are less carefully thought out than in the

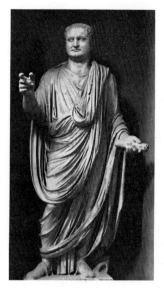

7.2　Titus, *c.* AD 80, height 196 cm, Vatican Museum, Rome.

7.3　Sabina (wife of emperor Hadrian) as Venus, *c.* AD 130, height 180 cm, Museo Ostiense, Ostia.

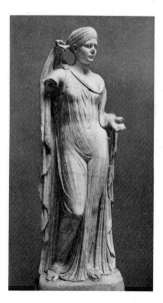

Spear-bearer, and the back is not even finished. Perhaps this is why the accomplished sculptor who carved this statue did not mind destroying Polykleitos' contrapposto by raising the shoulder on the same side as the raised hip. The balance of the torso is somewhat obscured anyway by the armour and the cloak, and in the front view the curve of the raised arm responds handsomely to the curve of the relaxed leg on the opposite side. The internal balance and self-contained rhythm of the classical statue have been lost, but a new rhythm, one which captured the authority of the imperial subject, was created.

Thus the Spear-bearer was transformed into Augustus; the classic structure has been Romanized. Enough of Polykleitos' invention is preserved to give the image an air of naturalness, dignity, and apparent inevitability, while the modifications have turned it into a fitting image of the first Roman emperor. This was a brilliant compromise, one that was very characteristic of the achievements of Roman art.

ROMAN PORTRAITS AND GREEK FORMS

A portrait of the later emperor Titus (AD 79–81) (7.2) seems more emphatically Roman. Titus is shown wearing the traditional Roman toga, a huge more-or-less oval garment that fell in a multitude of voluminous folds and required considerable skill to be draped properly. The specificity of the characterization is marked. No idealized Greek beauty tempers the crude features of the emperor, who, we may be surprised to find out, was considered the darling of mankind and praised for his good looks!

Yet the lessons learned from classical Greek art have not been forgotten or neglected. The technique of carving by which the pose of the body is revealed through the way the folds of the drapery fall was invented by the sculptors of the fifth century BC (compare 1.29, 2.19 and 7.6); its application to the portrait of the emperor is the Roman contribution.

A further example of the persistence of Greek ideas and forms is the portrait of Sabina, wife of the emperor Hadrian (117–138) (7.3). The body of the statue is simply a copy of the famous fifth-century-

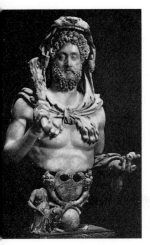

7.4 Commodus as
Hercules, last quarter of
the 2nd century AD,
height 141 cm, Museo
dei Conservatori, Rome.

BC 'Venus Genetrix' (1.29), but Roman modesty has made the sculptor cover the left breast. The statue, with the portrait head of Sabina set on top of the classical image of Venus, is a visual allegory. In Roman legend, the goddess Venus was supposed to be the mother of Aeneas, ancestor of the Roman people. This portrait of Sabina suggested that she had the same maternal relationship to the Roman populace of the time as the goddess had in the mythical past.

Allegory is also an element in the brilliantly carved portrait of the disagreeable emperor Commodus (180–192) (7.4). Commodus is draped in the lion-skin of Hercules (the Latin name of Herakles) and carries the hero's club in one hand and the apples of immortality in the other (compare the Atlas metope from Olympia, 2.14). Alexander the Great had been portrayed in the guise of Herakles, whom he claimed as founder of his line, and some Hellenistic kings had followed his example. Here, at a distance of half a millennium, a Roman emperor is doing the same.

The smooth surfaces of Commodus' skin are polished till they gleam, contrasting with the rich play of light and shadow in the hair and beard. Heavy-lidded, immaculately groomed, with an air of incontestable superiority, the emperor gazes out from beneath his Herculean disguise. This brutal ruler acted out the hero's role in hideous parody. Having collected all the legless inhabitants of Rome, he fitted these unfortunates with serpent-like trappings attached to the stumps of their limbs, gave them sponges to hurl instead of rocks, and slew them mercilessly with his club, declaring that he was Hercules punishing the obstreperous giants. This brilliant portrait, while preserving the official dignity of the emperor's image, still manages to hint at the character of the perverted sadist who occupied the position.

HISTORICAL RELIEFS: SPECIFICITY OF EVENT

The craving for specificity that we see in Roman portraits is also apparent in Roman reliefs. The most characteristic of these are the historical reliefs that were carved to decorate monuments erected to commemorate particular events (altars, arches, columns). Greek architectural sculpture (chap. 2) usually depicted timeless myths;

87

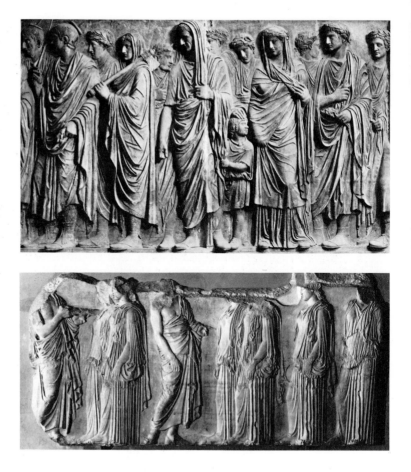

7.5 Part of the procession from the Ara Pacis, 13–9 BC, height 155 cm, Rome.

7.6 Part of the frieze from the Parthenon, 442–438 BC, height 106 cm, Louvre, Paris.

even the Parthenon frieze, which was in its own way commemorative, lacks the explicitness and specificity of person and event that was apparently necessary and meaningful to the Romans.

The Altar of Peace (Ara Pacis) that was erected by Augustus (31 BC–AD 14) demonstrates the Roman attitude. As was typical of Augustan art (see the Augustus from Prima Porta, 7.1), Greek models were used to impart dignity and grace to the subject, but Roman ideas pervade the whole.

The altar was richly decorated with reliefs. Some of them showed a procession (7.5) which certainly called to mind the procession carved on the Parthenon frieze (7.6). The beautiful play of light on the folds, the clear articulation of the bodies under the drapery, the wonderful sense of rhythmic progress – all these owe much to the forms of the Parthenon frieze. But, whereas on the Parthenon individuals cannot be identified (see 2.18 for several well-preserved heads) nor the exact moment determined, on the Ara Pacis

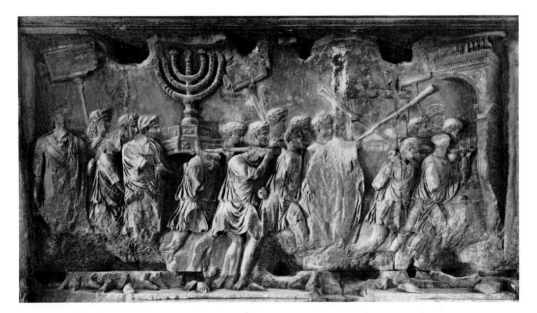

recognizable portraits are carved and the procession itself can be dated to the day (4 July 13 BC, though the carving was finished only four years later).

The uniqueness of the participants and of the event – it was the inauguration of the altar itself – is stressed; the priests in front wear their special spiked hats, a man with veiled head follows them carrying the axe to kill the sacrificial animals; then comes the tall general Agrippa to whose robes a timid child clings – all this is very different from the non-specific representations of classical art.

The decoration on the arch of Titus (7.7), like the portrait of Titus (7.2), seems less dependent on classical prototypes than do the reliefs and portraits carved for Augustus. The panel showing Titus' soldiers carrying the spoils from Jerusalem is particularly vivid. Since Roman sculpture and relief, like Greek, was always coloured, the carvings representing golden objects looted from the temple would have been gilded. Imagine how convincing this procession would have been when the soldiers' tunics were still brightly painted and the golden candlestick glittered against a painted dark blue sky. Much space and air has been left uncarved above the heads of the figures, and this gives the impression that they have much greater freedom of movement, in a more natural setting, than the members of the procession on the Ara Pacis, most of whose heads touch the confining top of the frieze (7.5).

A very different approach is used in the wonderfully delicate low

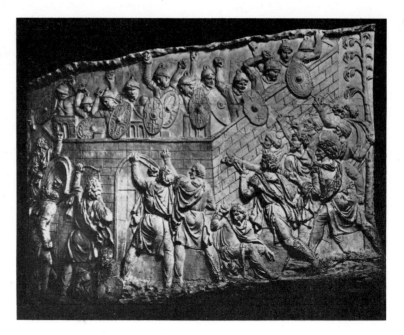

7.8 Romans attacked by barbarians, column of Trajan, Rome, AD 113, height of frieze *c.* 100 cm.

reliefs that decorate the great column commemorating the victories of the emperor Trajan (AD 98–117) over the Dacians (7.8). Quite another sort of realism is used here, not the vivid visual realism of the arch of Titus, but instead a sort of documentary, diagrammatic realism, conceptual truth being preferred to the truth that the eye sees.

The Romans are confined within their well-built camp, beating off the attack of the barbarian Dacians (7.8). Light-armed Dacian troops carrying bows and arrows and slings threaten the camp from the front and the right. Helmeted Romans within the camp hurl missiles down on the besiegers from the top of the wall. Though perfectly intelligible, the whole scene lacks visual logic. The Dacians are seen straight on at eye level; the Roman camp and the placement of its defenders are seen from above, though the Romans themselves are seen straight on. The walls of the camp have been made ridiculously low so that the artist could focus attention on the interesting combatants. Had he tried to keep all the elements in the scene in correct proportion, he would have had to devote most of his space to the depiction of immense dull stretches of wall and would have had to make the men tiny.

The conceptual (as opposed to visual) approach in the reliefs on the column of Trajan enables the artist to show complex action

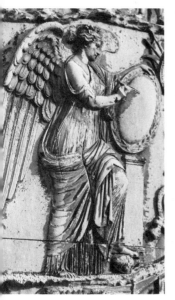

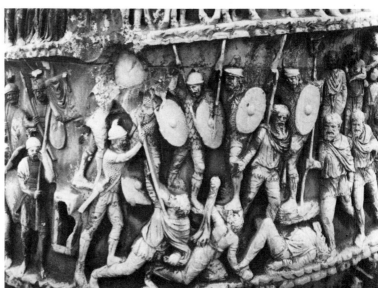

above
7.9 Victory writing on
a shield, column of
Trajan, Rome, AD 113,
height of frieze
c. 100 cm.

above right
7.10 Massacre of
barbarians, column of
Marcus Aurelius, Rome,
AD 180–193, height of
frieze *c.* 130 cm.

clearly by means of a certain amount of schematization. This seems very different from anything we have seen in Greek art, which insists on visual logic and consistency of presentation. And yet, even within the brilliantly original carving of the column of Trajan, tribute is paid to the fame and authority of Greek art. The interlude between the two campaigns that made up the Dacian wars is marked on the column by the figure of Victory (7.9) inscribing Trajan's triumph on a shield. Does she look familiar? She is none other than the much-loved Aphrodite of Capua (4.3), dressed up for the part, and equipped with wings.

Less than a century after the column decorated with reliefs was erected to glorify Trajan, another column was erected and carved in honour of Marcus Aurelius (161–180). Work on it continued throughout the reign of Marcus Aurelius' son Commodus (180–191). Like the portrait of Commodus (7.4) the sculpture on this column is revealing; at the same time, it is more emotional and expressive in style than the carvings on the column of Trajan.

A characteristic relief (7.10) shows the massacre of barbarians. A harsh and brutal contrast is made between the armed and aggressive Romans at the top stabbing down mercilessly on their unarmed foes, and the helpless, pleading barbarians, fallen or dead. The man slightly to the right of centre who throws back his arms and screams in horror captures the mood of the scene.

The relief is much more deeply cut than that on the column of Trajan (7.8 and 7.9) and as deficient in subtlety of modelling as it is lacking in correctness of drawing (notice how unnaturally long are the legs and body of the Roman at the left). The carving, though highly expressive, has none of the smooth skill that was mustered for the portrait of Commodus (7.4). Troubled times that were now overwhelming the empire had affected the spirit of the people and the sculptors working on the column. The work here heralds that breakdown of style and decline in skill which was to be characteristic of most sculpture (with the exception of portrait sculpture) during the third century AD.

RELIEFS FOR PRIVATE INDIVIDUALS: SARCOPHAGI

Little official sculpture was produced for the State after the first quarter of the third century; the government had other things to worry about than the erection of commemorative monuments. Between the years 235 and 285 some twenty-six emperors reigned, constantly threatened by usurpers. Only one died a natural death. Civil war plagued the empire, while at the same time the barbarians were hammering on the frontiers.

Many people hoped for better times in the life to come, and those who could afford it ordered elaborate carved coffins (*sarcophagi*) in which to have their bodies entombed. The fashion for burial in sarcophagi had begun around the middle of the second century and grew considerably in the difficult period of the third century. Sarcophagi and portraits were almost the only kinds of sculpture produced then.

Sarcophagi were decorated in several different ways. Sometimes the relief carvings on them illustrated Greek myths, sometimes Roman battles, sometimes typical incidents from the life of the deceased; sometimes they were ornamented with representations of the seasons, or scenes of Bacchic delight, or just lush hanging garlands.

Few of these sarcophagi are artistic masterpieces. They are, however, very important for the history of art, for many of them survived from antiquity or were found in the Renaissance, when

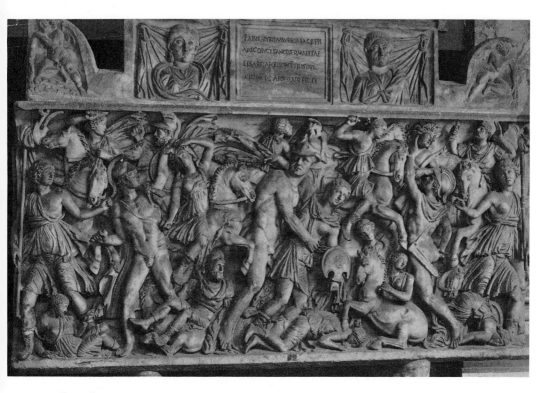

7.11 Sarcophagus
showing Achilles and
Penthesilea, mid 3rd
century AD, height
117 cm, Vatican
Museum, Rome.

they were extravagantly admired and proved a great source of
inspiration to artists.

A mid-third-century sarcophagus (7.11) that was much appreciated during the Renaissance depicts on its front the story of
Achilles and Penthesilea. Penthesilea was queen of the Amazons, a
legendary band of warrior women. According to the myth, the
Amazons were allies of the Trojans and came to fight beside them
when the Greeks were attacking the city. Achilles, the champion of
the Greeks, fought the Amazon queen in single combat and killed
her. His triumph, however, was hollow for, as she expired, he
realized that he had fallen in love with her.

The sarcophagus shows Achilles prominently in the centre,
holding the lifeless body of Penthesilea. Around them the battle
continues to rage. Warriors, male and female, and their horses fill
the entire height of the sarcophagus. Some of the figures are tiny;
others nearly as large as Achilles. At either side a large Amazon flees,
but turns her head to look back. The two are mirror images of each
other. Their formal symmetry, so at odds with the disorder of the
battle, gives a clue to the principle of design used in the carving of
the sarcophagus: it is meant to be decorative. The artist thought that

93

enough of the story was conveyed by the central group. He used the other figures as fillers, shrunken in size or enlarged as necessary in order to make the entire panel a rippling surface of lights and shadows. He was interested neither in composing a plausibly naturalistic scene nor in telling a story convincingly. What the artist was searching for was an over-all decorative pattern not too different in aesthetic aim from the geometric vase painted by a Greek artist a thousand years before (3.3).

Roman sculpture, then, lay under heavy debt to Greek sculpture. Original Roman contributions were stimulated by characteristically Roman demands for representations of particular people and events and led to new creations in portraiture and the carving of documentary, commemorative reliefs. But from the end of the second century, an increasing interest in expression and decoration began to draw the Romans away from the rationality and restraint that had always been a part of Greek sculpture.

8 Roman painting

below
8.1 Roman wall painting, copy of a Greek original, showing Perseus freeing Andromeda, 1st century AD, height 122 cm, Museo Nazionale, Naples.

below right
8.2 Roman wall painting, copy of the same Greek original as 8.1, showing Perseus freeing Andromeda, 1st century AD, height 38 cm, Museo Nazionale, Naples.

GREEK INSPIRATION FOR ROMAN PAINTING

The Romans admired Greek painting as much as they admired Greek sculpture, and encouraged the artists they employed to make copies of particularly famous or popular Greek works for them (8.1 and 8.2). Single figures, groups and entire panel paintings were reproduced, adapted, spoiled or beautified according to the ability of the painters and the demands of the patrons.

While Greek painting has been largely lost, a great deal of Roman painting has survived. Most of what we have comes from the walls of private houses and public buildings in Pompeii and Herculaneum, two provincial but fashionable towns that were buried when Vesuvius erupted in AD 79. A few other paintings have also been found in Rome and elsewhere. It appears that the Romans decorated

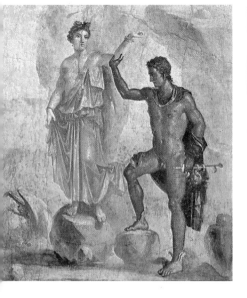

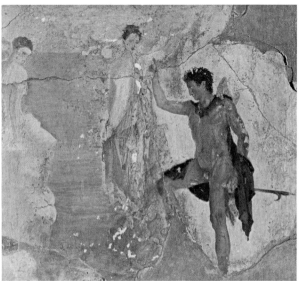

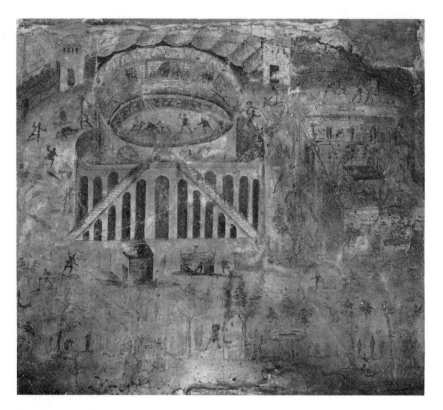

8.3 Roman wall painting from Pompeii showing the riot in and around the amphitheatre in AD 59, third quarter of the 1st century AD, height 170 cm, Museo Nazionale, Naples.

their walls with mural paintings much more frequently than did the Greeks.

The impression given by this abundant material is generally attractive, occasionally beautiful, but taken as a whole second-rate and derivative.

AN EXAMPLE OF A THOROUGHLY ROMAN PAINTING

Some paintings seem independent of the pervasive Greek influence. One such is a lively portrayal of a riot in the amphitheatre in Pompeii (8.3). This was a real event: a fight broke out between the Pompeians and visitors from nearby Nocera in AD 59 and the disturbance was so great that the emperor ordered the amphitheatre closed for ten years after the fray. The choice of subject is very Roman, as is the visually illogical but intellectually lucid way in which it is portrayed.

The oval interior of the amphitheatre is seen from a bird's eye view; the figures within it head-on and over-large. The exterior is

96

drawn in a frontal view. The great triangle in front is the support for the flights of stairs that led up the outside of the amphitheatre and over the top to the seating inside. The artist has helpfully turned the staircases outwards so that the steps can be seen. Actually, of course, they would not have been visible from the angle at which the rest of the exterior is shown. The whole picture reminds us of parts of the decoration on the column of Trajan.

The paintings that are copies of Greek originals (compare 8.1 and 8.2 and 5.5 and 5.6) look a great deal less naive than this Roman provincial scene.

ROMAN SETTINGS: THE FOUR POMPEIAN 'STYLES'

The Romans devoted great care to the painted settings in which they placed their copies of Greek paintings, and the complex and changing organization of their painted walls makes an absorbing study.

Scholars have divided the decoration of Pompeian walls into four 'styles'. The *first style*, one that was common throughout the Mediterranean world during the second century BC, was hardly a matter of painting at all. It consisted simply of covering the wall with plaster painted and shaped to look like different kinds of marble slabs. It was supposed to make the whole wall appear as if veneered with expensive foreign marbles, which is presumably the way palaces were decorated.

About the beginning of the first century BC, some Roman painters discovered that they did not have to make the plaster protrude physically to give the impression of three-dimensional blocks; they could paint the wall illusionistically to give the same effect.

Once the idea of illusion had dawned, a radical change took place in the style. If one could paint the illusion of protruding blocks, why not paint the illusion of open windows and distant landscapes, people, animals, birds and gardens?

Thus was born the *second style*. It was an original Roman creation. Second-style walls were painted to suggest either that the confines of the room had been pushed back or that they had been totally removed. Sometimes a parapet is painted upon which figures stand

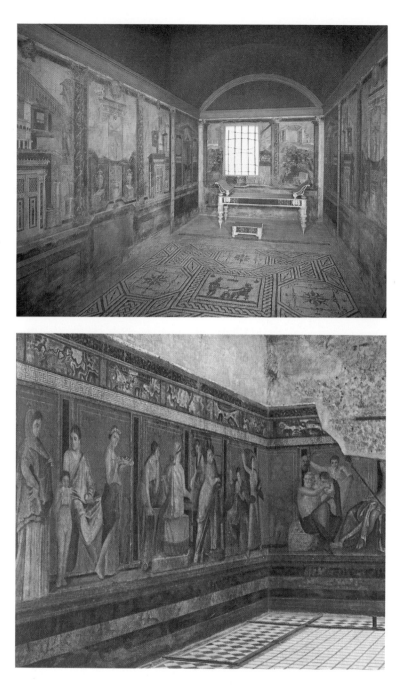

8.4 Second-style room
from Boscoreale, Roman
wall paintings of *c.* 40 BC,
dimensions of the room
436 × 656 cm,
Metropolitan Museum
of Art, New York,
Rogers Fund, 1903.

8.5 Second-style room
from the Villa of the
Mysteries, mid 1st
century BC, height (of
figures) *c.* 150 cm,
Pompeii

or sit (8.5); sometimes a colonnade is painted through which one can
see distant views (8.4); sometimes the whole space above the parapet
is illusionistically opened up and the walls of the room are made to
resemble a charming garden. The illusions are always rational and

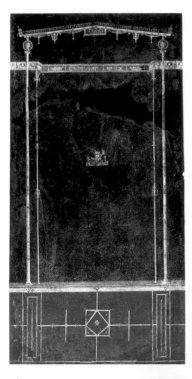

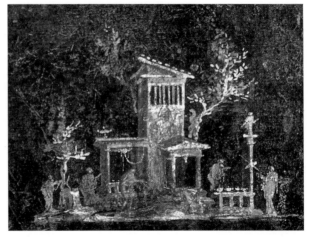

8.7 Detail of third-style wall from Boscotrecase (8.6), floating landscape.

above
8.6 Third-style wall from Boscotrecase, Roman wall painting from the late 1st century BC, dimensions of the room 470 × 540 cm (preserved height 238 cm), Metropolitan Museum of Art, New York, Rogers Fund, 1920.

8.8a Fourth-style room in the house of the Vettii, Roman wall paintings from the third quarter of the 1st century AD, Pompeii (see p. 101 for a view of the whole).

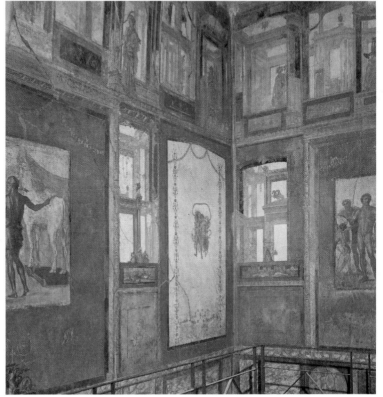

naturalistic, giving a plausible extension of the space, but they are deliciously varied.

A little room from a villa at Boscoreale (near Pompeii) was painted in the second style with views mostly into architectural vistas (8.4). The lowest part of the wall, the dado, is decorated rather simply with stripes and imitation flat marble panels. This is the part of the wall that might easily be obscured by furniture or damaged in cleaning. Above it there is a painted ledge on which some red columns appear to stand. Between the columns there is a view of city streets on either side of an enclosed sanctuary. It is as if one looked out of a small room into a spacious, delightful scene beyond.

The farthest section of the room is separated by tall white pilasters which extend all the way to the floor. Above the dado on the back wall there is a charming landscape and, on either side, views of shrines. Despite much formal symmetry, the vistas seem perfectly possible, even though we know that most (if not all) of the scenes are copies of Greek prototypes (5.5).

Sometimes the illusionistic extension of the room does not penetrate so far. In the celebrated Villa of the Mysteries at Pompeii, the bottom section of the wall is treated in the same way as in the little room from Boscoreale, but on the platform, instead of columns which give onto a distant vista, there are figures who perform the ritual associated with a cult of Dionysus in front of a flat crimson wall (8.5).

This visually logical and plausible style began to pall by the last decade or so of the first century BC, and artists and patrons began to look for something new. This led to the invention of the *third style*, one which emphasized the flat confining nature of the walls, delighted in delicate and sophisticated details, and outspokenly denied all appearances of rationality and logic.

An enchanting example of the third style comes from a villa at Boscotrecase (also near Pompeii) that was owned by members of the imperial family and presumably shows what were the most up-to-date and elegant fashions. The whole wall is painted black (8.6). Above the dado there is an extremely narrow ledge on which two pairs of impossibly thin columns stand. The outer, sturdier columns hold up a delicate gable from which pearls and gems seem to dangle. It is a sort of jeweller's architecture, rich, fanciful and exquisite. The

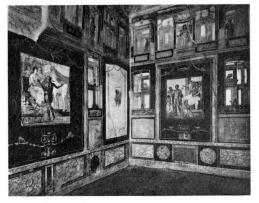

8.8b Fourth-style room in the house of the Vettii, Roman wall paintings from the third quarter of the 1st century AD, Pompeii (see p. 99 for a detail in colour).

inner columns support a frieze that looks as if it were a beautifully embroidered ribbon.

In the centre of the flat, black spaceless wall there is a little landscape (detail, 8.7). It is convincingly three-dimensional – the deft treatment of light gives a vivid impression of depth – but it floats in mid-air in a most unlikely manner. The black background of the wall can be interpreted either as flat and spaceless or as deep and spacious. The illuminated landscape accentuates this ambiguity and playfully foils any attempts at rational analysis.

By AD 62, when Pompeii was shaken by an earthquake and many houses had to be redecorated, most people had tired of the third style. Once again they wanted paintings that created the illusion of space and appeared to open out the confining walls of their often very small rooms. In the *fourth style* they tried to create a new synthesis between second-style spaciousness and third-style elegance.

A room in the Pompeian 'house of the Vettii' gives a good example of fourth-style decoration (8.8). In the centre of each wall there is a flat red panel framing a square painting (usually a copy of a Greek work). On either side of and above this red panel, the wall appears to be opened up to allow for a view into the distance. The expansive views are distinctly theatrical, and in this differ from the everyday views of the second style. The side walls are treated the same way as the back walls, but, as they are longer, there is space for an additional white panel. This panel is painted in the third style, with a delicate border and a pair of figures floating in an unlikely manner in the middle of the white nothingness, which can be interpreted either as airy space or as flat wall.

This rather vulgarly painted room gives an idea of the general level of painting at Pompeii: cheerful, but rather crude. The central pictures are fashionable, but usually insensitive, copies of Greek

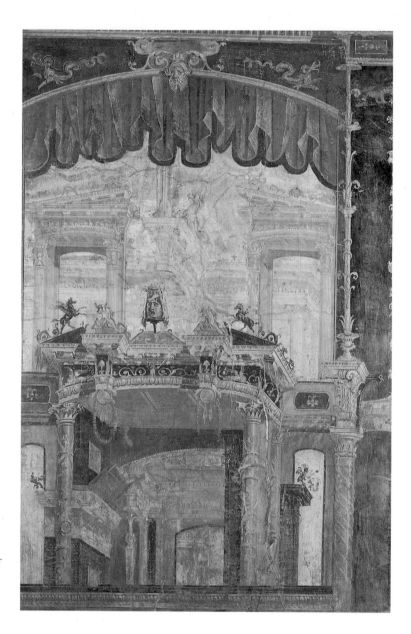

8.9 Fragment of
fourth-style decoration
from Herculaneum,
Roman wall painting
from the third quarter of
the 1st century AD,
height 195 cm, Museo
Nazionale, Naples.

models and some rather flashy effects are sought in the theatrical
views. A fragment that we have of a far finer painting (8.9) must have
been placed fairly high on the left-hand side of a wall scheme like
that in the house of the Vettii (8.8), judging from the angle suggested
by the perspective. The delicacy of the painting, the sureness of
tonal range and the bravura make this theatrical vista the equal of
any of the masterpieces of baroque decorative painting, sixteen
centuries later.

9 Roman architecture: adaptation and evolution

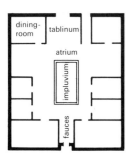

9.1a Plan of a traditional Roman atrium house.

9.1b Plan of a Roman house with the traditional atrium in front and a peristyle added at the back.

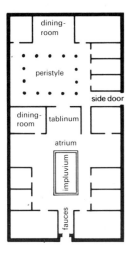

The Romans built houses and temples long before they came into contact with the Greeks and had strong, old, and sanctified traditions as to how these should be constructed.

The traditional Roman house, unlike the Greek house, was built according to a strict and invariable plan (9.1 a). It was entered through a door placed in the centre of the short side, giving it from the outset a strong sense of a central axis that was totally lacking in the more casual Greek houses (6.1a–c). The entrance (*fauces*) led into the *atrium*, a great central space with a rectangular opening in the roof which let in light and air (rain, too, which was collected in a basin – the *impluvium* – connected to a subterranean cistern). On a direct line with the fauces, on the opposite side of the atrium, was the *tablinum*, the main room in which the master of the house presided. The rest of the rooms opened off the atrium in an arrangement that was less rigorously prescribed, though always basically symmetrical.

When the Romans encountered the Greeks during the Hellenistic period and fell under the spell of their superior culture, they could not fail to admire the charm and flexibility of Greek houses. They were particularly impressed by the gracious peristyles which were by then a feature of the courtyard of many Greek houses (6.1 c).

The Romans had great respect for tradition and were unwilling to alter the traditional form of their houses, which served important functions within their society; yet they wished to incorporate some of the qualities they admired in Greek houses. The solution they arrived at is so simple that it is almost mechanical (9.1b.). They continued to build the front part of their houses in the traditional manner, but added onto the back – the more private part of the house – a Greek type of peristyle with rooms casually arranged around it.

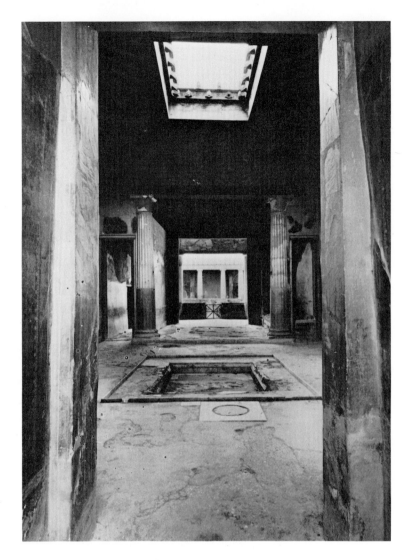

9.2 View from the fauces through the atrium into the peristyle of a house (the House of the Menander) in Pompeii, 1st century BC.

On the plan, this new type of Roman house may not look very exciting, but in fact the play of light and shadow, the contrast of the illuminated atrium, dark tablinum, and light-filled peristyle beyond, make for a very beautiful and striking effect (9.2). Notice, too, the sense of order, the axial build-up to a climax, which much resembles the principles of planning that underlay the sanctuary of Fortuna at Praeneste (6.6).

Tradition also dictated the form of the Roman temple. Following Etruscan precedent, temples were normally built on a high podium, accessible only by a flight of steps in front (9.3). The cella (the main room of the temple, which might be single or divided into three

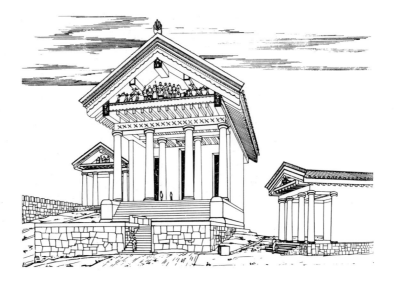

9.3 Drawing of a traditional Etruscan–early Roman type of temple.

parts) covered the full width of the podium and also reached all the way to the back. The only part of the podium not covered by the cella was at the front, where a deep porch led from the top of the flight of steps into the cella. Both the plan and the elevation of a Roman temple were different from the Greek (2.1a–d, 2.2 and 2.3).

A Greek temple was normally not set very high; it was usually supported all round on just three steps. By contrast a Roman temple on its high podium towered above everyone approaching it (9.3). A Greek temple generally looked much the same from all four sides; not so a Roman temple. The front, which was accentuated by the flight of steps and the porch, looked strikingly different from the sides, which were of little importance, and the back, which was negligible. The back, in fact, was so unimportant that it was often built against a wall. Thus the Roman temple could become attached (like a relief) rather than remaining a free-standing building.

When the Romans became acquainted with the Greeks, they began to improve the appearance of their temples along Greek lines, but, as in the matter of the house, they did not violate traditional usages. Once again a compromise solution was found, and it is well illustrated in the Augustan temple that was built at Nîmes in southern France (9.4).

The Romans were more struck by the external peristyles of Greek temples than by any other feature, so it was this handsome embellishment that they tried to apply to their traditional type of temple. From the plan (9.5) it is obvious that the characteristic form of the Roman temple has been preserved, that the temple is set on a

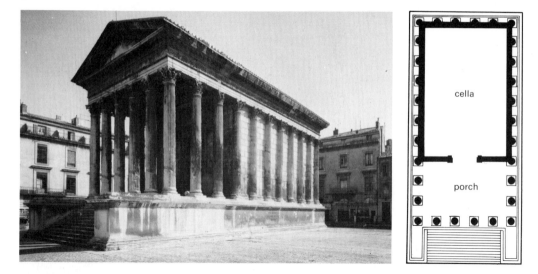

cella

porch

above
9.4   The Maison
Carrée, a Roman temple
with partially attached
peristyle, late 1st
century BC, Nîmes,
France.

above right
9.5   Plan of the Maison
Carrée, Nîmes (9.4).

high podium, accessible only by steps at the front, and that the cella,
preceded by a deep porch, extends all the way across and to the back
of the podium. The great innovation was the extension of the porch
colonnade all round the temple so that it appears to be encircled by a
peristyle. The full round columns of the porch had to be squashed
into attached half-columns (engaged columns) when they were
forced to share the edge of the podium with the outer walls of the
cella (9.4). Compromises are seldom perfect; still, this was a good
one, made in much the same spirit as the statue of Augustus from
Prima Porta (7.1), with which it is contemporary.

A Greek temple was best approached from one corner (2.3), for
this approach immediately reveals the principal dimensions of the
temple and establishes its independence as a free-standing building.
Gateways in Greek sanctuaries were generally arranged so that the
worshippers' first view of a Greek temple was from this angle (6.5).
For the Roman temple, however, this view is less satisfying (9.4).
The abrupt change from free-standing colonnade to attached
columns where the walls of the cella intrude on the illusion of a
peristyle is disturbing.

Consequently, the layout of Roman sanctuaries and precincts
usually obliged visitors to take up a position directly opposite the
front of a temple. There is a feeling of inevitable rightness once one
stands facing the temple at Nîmes on its axis (9.6). The flight of steps
invites one to mount (while the high podium approached from any
other angle discourages further advance) and the shady porch draws
one in. The tall façade looming up with strong vertical emphasis

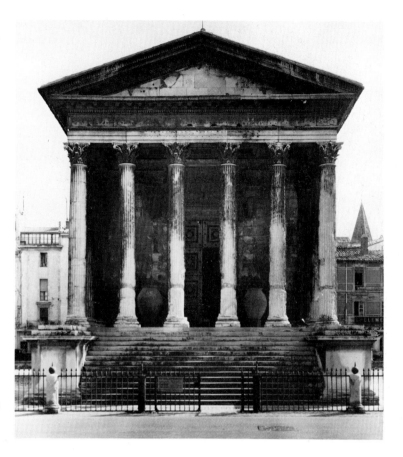

9.6 The Maison Carrée (same as 9.4) seen from the correct angle.

dominates the space in front of it, just as the statue of Augustus from Prima Porta (7.1) with its powerfully raised arm dominates the space before it.

Not all Roman temples show this compromise between Roman tradition and Greek trappings. Some were remarkably original. One of the most amazing is the Pantheon, built in Rome in the time of the emperor Hadrian (117–138) and fortunately still extremely well preserved.

The architect of the Pantheon (who may have been the emperor himself) draws on old Roman traditions, techniques, and materials to create something dazzlingly new. Circular as well as rectangular temples had been built in Rome from ancient times. Inside, circular temples were cramped cylinders. The vast uncluttered, domed interior of the Pantheon (9.7), breathtaking in its serenity and grandeur, was quite novel. The height of the dome is equal to the diameter of the base, so that the great hemisphere tranquilly resting upon the ample drum seems to shape a sphere of space. The circular

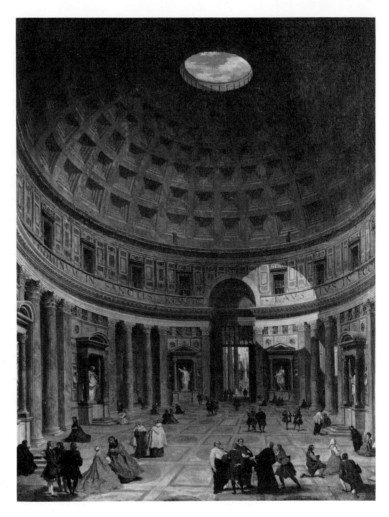

9.7 Interior of the Pantheon, a second-century AD Roman round temple, painting by Pannini in the 18th century AD, National Gallery of Art, Washington DC, Samuel H. Kress Collection.

opening in the centre of the dome floods the building with light and throws a moving circle of sunshine on the walls. An eighteenth-century painting shows the rich inlays of marble that lined the interior. (Possibly it was effects of this sort that wall painters in the first Pompeian style were striving to capture, p. 97.)

Only a dome could roof the great central space of the Pantheon without requiring intermediate supports. By the second century AD the Romans had amassed considerable experience in building arches, vaults, and domes. They used them in numerous works of practical and ornamental architecture. An arch is built of wedge-shaped stones (*voussoirs*) which become self-supporting once the key-stone is in place. Until then it has to be built on a framework (*centring*) of wood. An arch extended in length becomes a barrel vault; an arch that is rotated becomes a dome. The structural principles are the same for all three forms.

The dome of the Pantheon does not require a key-stone because it is built of concrete, which, once set, is self-supporting. Knowledge of how to build arches and vaults was necessary for its construction, as was also a huge wooden centring, but the final form was possible only because of the Romans' experience and skill in the use of concrete.

The Romans began to use concrete in the second century BC. It was cheap, strong, and malleable and could be used for huge projects, such as the sanctuary of Fortuna at Praeneste (6.6), where the whole side of a hill was transformed into an architectural complex. Buildings of concrete were constructed as follows: two low walls were built (if below ground, between wooden shutters; if above ground, of mortared bricks). The space between the walls was filled with broken stones (aggregate). Then the fluid concrete was poured in. It flowed around the pieces of stone that made up the aggregate and bonded with the mortar that held the bricks in the two containing walls together. Then it hardened. As soon as it was dry enough, the containing walls were built to a higher level, more aggregate was laid between them and a new batch of concrete was poured in. As the building rose, the nature of the aggregate was altered. Heavy stones were used at the bottom, lighter ones as the walls grew higher. Very light materials, like pumice, would be used in the aggregate of a dome, for which a wooden centring would have to be employed.

The shape of the final concrete building was defined by the shape of the containing walls between which the aggregate was laid. Since the Romans usually used rather small bricks or, alternatively, carpented wood to construct these walls, they could be flexibly and imaginatively curved. Furthermore, concrete could take the shape of anything that was pressed against it before it dried. Thus wooden moulds were used to make the coffers in the dome of the Pantheon (9.7). Once the concrete had set, the moulds were removed but the shape remained. The coffers make a great aesthetic contribution to the appearance of the dome, for they make its sphericity apparent, defining the curve and the recession by means of light and shadow and subtly used perspective. A smooth dome, evenly flooded with

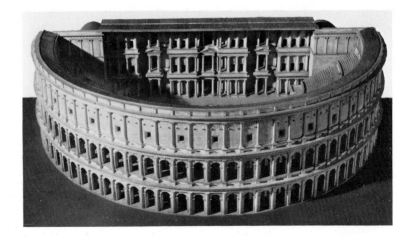

9.8 Model of the theatre of Marcellus, Rome, late 1st century BC.

light, as the dome of the Pantheon is, would just look flat. Notice how undefined even the central portion of the Pantheon's dome is where there is no coffering to throw shadows.

FROM THEATRE TO AMPHITHEATRE

Engineering experience in the use of arches and vaults, and practical experience in the use of concrete, enabled the Romans to create buildings in shapes and on a scale that could never have been dreamed of by the Greeks. Such techniques also enabled them to transform the Greek theatre. Greek theatres were built into hillsides (6.2); they were not free-standing buildings. The Romans ingeniously used tiers of arches made out of concrete to construct the equivalent of a hillside on which to rest the seats of the auditorium. Thus they were able to build theatres anywhere, even in the flattest stretches of desert, and the theatres they built were free-standing and independent (9.8).

The Romans gave their theatres an appearance of unity and coherence by erecting a scene building (*scaenae frons*: plural *scaenae frontes*) that was as tall as the top of the auditorium and connected with it. Thus the semi-circular area of the theatre was completely enclosed, and the three originally distinct parts of the Greek theatre (6.2) were welded into a single unit (9.9).

Spectacles in the theatre were addressed to the audience. Actors would stand with their backs to the scaenae frons and direct their speeches to the crowds that only partially encircled them. Other entertainments that the Romans enjoyed did not have any such built-in, necessary sense of direction. The bloody fights of

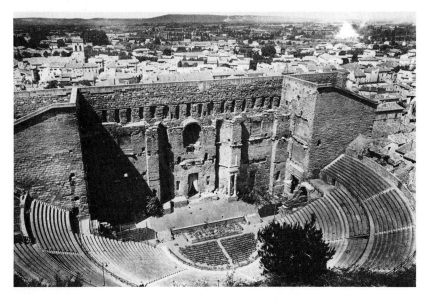

9.9 Roman theatre, 1st century AD, Orange, France.

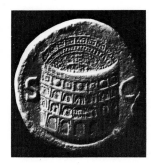

9.10 The Colosseum as shown on a coin minted AD 238–244.

gladiators, or men against wild beasts, or wild beasts against each other, like modern bullfights or football games, did not have to be viewed from any one direction. In fact they were better viewed from all round.

The Romans created an architectural form to fit the need. The invention has the simplicity of genius: two theatres were placed back to back and the intervening walls of the scaenae frontes removed. What resulted was an oval arena encased in an oval of tiered seats; not a theatre but an *amphi*theatre. The coin (9.10) which shows a representation of the most famous of all amphitheatres, the Colosseum in Rome, conveys in a single glance the essentials of the structure. Like the painting of the riot in the amphitheatre in Pompeii (8.3) and some of the carvings on the column of Trajan (7.8) visual realism has been sacrificed for the sake of diagrammatic clarity. Thus one sees the interior of the amphitheatre and at the same time the exterior, which was built on superimposed tiers of arches. A combination of cut stone and concrete was used to construct this giant arena, the dedication of which was one of the principal events in the short reign of the emperor Titus (79–81). It was not the first amphitheatre – the one in Pompeii was earlier – but it was probably the finest. The arcades of the exterior were filled with sculptures. These have long been lost, but the fact that they once existed gives an indication of what an immense quantity of sculpture was produced during the period of the Roman empire.

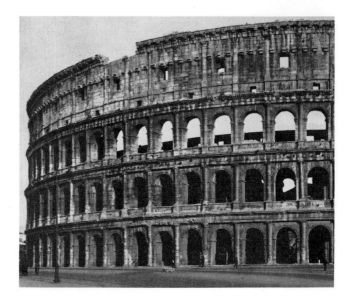

9.11 Exterior of the Colosseum (the Flavian amphitheatre), inaugurated AD 80.

Greek theatres (from which the Colosseum is derived at two removes), having been built into the sides of hills, had no exteriors; the Colosseum, by contrast, had a gigantic one. Much thought was given to its decoration (9.11). In addition to the statues placed within the arches, a veneer of Greek orders is superimposed on the arcades. On the lowest register, attached Doric half-columns support an attached architrave; on the second register, there are attached Ionic half-columns; on the third, attached Corinthian half-columns, and at the top, which was added later, attached Corinthian pilasters. These orders support nothing. They are not structural, but ornamental. This does not mean they were unimportant.

The application of these orders served two functions. First, they clearly allude to Greek architecture. This was the way the Romans showed their appreciation of Greek culture. Adding Greek orders to the exterior of a theatre or an amphitheatre was rather like adding a Greek peristyle to a Roman type of temple (9.4–9.6), a touch of Greek elegance that did not affect the basic Roman structure underneath.

Second, the application of the orders gave the impression of scaling down the building, making it more accessible to human beings without diminishing its tremendous size. The naked, unarticulated structure of the Colosseum, the superimposed tiers of arcades (9.12), is gigantic, dwarfing any people who might approach it. Roman architects wanted Roman citizens to appreciate the

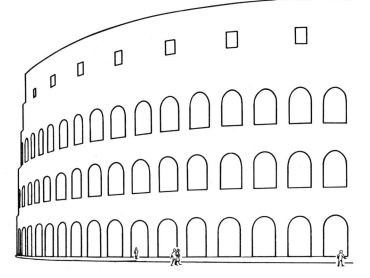

9.12 Drawing of the Colosseum, showing the structure alone without the addition of the applied orders.

grandeur of their creations, but they also wanted them to feel that they shared in that grandeur, not that they were tiny and insignificant. Faced with the great mass of the building an individual might have been daunted; however, since the orders have been applied, one does not have to relate to the whole building, but merely to a single bay. Notice in 9.12 how small a person is in relation to the entire structure, but how much larger he seems (9.11) when he is measured only against the rectangle described by the columns and architrave that frame a single arch. In this way a Roman citizen could feel himself a significant part of the huge building and of the huge empire that it represented.

WORLD ARCHITECTURE FOR WORLD RULERS

The Romans were great organizers and great builders. Wherever they went, and they went all over the western part of the civilized world, they established colonies and built cities. These contained theatres, amphitheatres and temples, all recognizably on the models we have looked at. They can be found throughout Europe, in many parts of North Africa and in western Asia. Techniques of vaulting and of building with concrete spread with the spread of the Roman empire. Even in the eastern part of the empire, where the Hellenistic tradition remained strong and cities had been large and well appointed for a long time, new buildings were erected following Roman models and old ones were modified to accommodate a more Roman way of life.

Baths, law courts, government buildings, aqueducts, market places – all these and many other practical and ornamental edifices were produced by the Romans both at home and abroad. All are handled with skill and imagination, yet most are based on the same splendid metropolitan types.

In time, after the fall of the empire, these great constructions began to decay. Statues were looted and burned to produce lime, marble veneers were stolen from walls, and roofs fell in. Yet even in ruins the massive remains of what the Romans built still astound the visitor and stir his imagination.

Epilogue

Time, war, and vandalism have all contributed to the destruction of the art of Greece and Rome. Mere fragments have survived, and yet these have often proved inspiration enough for later ages.

Even as early as the Carolingian period, artists and thinkers began to look back to pagan antiquity for models of humanity and culture in art and literature. But it was only in the Renaissance (from the fifteenth century) that the art of Greece and Rome came to be fully appreciated in its own right. From that time on it has been ceaselessly studied, copied, admired and analysed. During the neo-classical period (the eighteenth century) people became increasingly aware of the differences between Greek art and Roman art, instead of lumping them together as 'classical antiquity', and this distinction has been refined ever since.

The newly emerging urban societies of the Renaissance were immensely impressed by what they learned of the urban societies of antiquity. For centuries the revival of antiquity seemed the highest possible goal for civilized man. Even plaster casts and humble Latin texts were enthusiastically used to open receptive eyes and minds to the glories of the past.

The twentieth century has other concerns. The intensity of the passion once felt for the art of Greece and Rome has faded, but the beauty and the power of the creations themselves remain, mute but eloquent testimony to the glory that was Greece and the grandeur that was Rome.

Notes on artists

AGATHARCHOS, fifth-century-BC Samian who worked in Athens and made scene paintings for dramatic performances; the first painter to use perspective on a large scale.

ARISTONOTHOS, seventh-century-BC potter who probably migrated from Greek southern Italy or Sicily to Etruscan Cerveteri; one of the earliest Greek artists to sign his work (3.5).

EUTHYMIDES, Athenian red-figure vase painter of the late sixth century BC (3.11).

EXEKIAS, Athenian potter and painter in the black-figure technique who worked during the third quarter of the sixth century BC (3.8).

KLEITIAS, Athenian black-figure vase painter of the second quarter of the sixth century BC, painter of the François vase (3.6).

MYRON, Athenian sculptor from Eleutherai, creator of the bronze Discus-thrower (1.18), who was active in the second quarter of the fifth century BC.

NIKIAS, Athenian panel painter of the fourth century BC who also painted some of the marble statues by Praxiteles.

PARRHASIOS, panel painter from Ephesus of late fifth to early fourth century BC who was noted for his suggestive and evocative use of contours.

PEIRAIKOS, Hellenistic painter of 'odds and ends'.

PHEIDIAS, Athenian sculptor of the second and third quarters of the fifth century BC who worked in bronze and marble, but was most celebrated for his huge chryselephantine statues of gods. He was the general overseer of work on the Parthenon and other Periclean projects and was instrumental in the creation of the high classical style.

POLYGNOTOS, Greek painter of the early classical period (second quarter of the fifth century BC) who was especially noted for his representations of quiet scenes and his revelation of character and mood. He seems to have been the first to set the figures in his large wall paintings on different levels, thereby suggesting that they existed in a deeper spatial setting than had ever been painted before.

POLYKLEITOS, Argive bronze-caster active in the second half of the fifth century BC (the high classical period); he wrote a book (now lost) on ideal proportions called the *Canon* and illustrated his theories by making the statue of the Spear-bearer (1.23). Roman copies of his works show fully developed contrapposto.

PRAXITELES, Athenian marble sculptor of mid-fourth century BC (who also worked in bronze) particularly celebrated for his representations of lyrical emotions (4.1).

SKOPAS, sculptor of mid fourth century BC from Paros particularly noted for representations of passionate states.

SOSOS OF PERGAMON, Hellenistic mosaicist (5.4).

ZEUXIS, Greek panel painter from Heraclea who lived in the late fifth and early fourth centuries BC, noted for his use of shading to give the illusion of solidity and three-dimensionality to his painted figures.

Glossary

ABACUS the topmost part of the capital: plain in Doric capitals, moulded in Ionic and Corinthian.

ACROTERIA (SINGULAR: acroterion) decorative ornaments placed above the three angles of the pediment on the front and the back of a temple.

ALABASTRON ovoid narrow-necked perfume holder (3.4).

AMPHITHEATRE oval Roman building with seating facing inwards onto a central area for gladiatorial or similar spectacles (8.3, 9.10, 9.11).

AMPHORA capacious storage jar with two handles (3.4).

ARCH curved masonry construction for spanning an opening.

ARCHAIC term referring to the early period of Greek art from about 650 to 490 BC.

ARCHITRAVE a lintel or beam carried from the top of one column to the top of another (also called *epistyle*).

ARYBALLOS small round container used by athletes to carry the oil they rubbed down with after exercise (3.4).

ATRIUM central hall of a Roman house of the traditional type (9.1a).

BASE lowest member of a column (2.6) (not used in the Doric order).

BLACK-FIGURE technique of vase painting in which the figures are drawn in black silhouette, details and internal markings are incised, and touches of white and purplish-red are added. (The technique was invented by the Corinthians in the seventh century BC and widely used throughout Greece in the sixth century BC. It continued to be used for special purposes as late as the second century BC.)

CAPITAL top part of a column, crowning the shaft and supporting the architrave.

CAVEA the place for spectators sitting in a Greek or Roman theatre (the auditorium).

CELLA the inner part of a Roman temple in which the image of the god was kept. Some temples which honoured three gods (the Capitoline Triad) had three cellas.

CENTRING a temporary (usually wooden) framework for supporting a masonry arch or vault during construction until it is able to stand by itself.

CHRYSELEPHANTINE statues that were plated with gold (for clothing) and ivory (for flesh parts).

CLASSICAL term referring to the period in Greek art from 480 to 323 BC. See also *early classical* and *high classical*. 'Late classical' (399–323 BC) is not used in this book.

COLUMN cylindrical support that consists of shaft and capital (and sometimes, as in the Ionic order, a base).

CONTRAPPOSTO balanced pose of a human figure in which the weight is unevenly distributed and the axis of the shoulders slopes in the opposite direction from the axis of the hips (1.23, 4.1, 4.2, for example).

CORINTHIAN CAPITAL a capital decorated with leaves and small volutes (2.8).

CORNICE the topmost member of the entablature.

DENTILS small carved tooth-like features used as an alternative to a continuous frieze in the Ionic order.

DORIANS people speaking the Dorian dialect of Greek and living chiefly on mainland Greece (the Peloponnese), the southern islands of the Aegean (including Crete and Rhodes) and the southern part of the west coast of Asia Minor.

DORIC ORDER an architectural system controlling the design of column and entablature (2.4).

EARLY CLASSICAL period from the end of the Persian wars (479 BC) to about the middle of the fifth century BC, during which the bronze-caster Myron and the painter Polygnotos were active and the sculptures of the temple of Zeus at Olympia were produced.

ENGAGED COLUMN OR HALF-COLUMN a column (more usually, a half-column, semi-circular in plan) that is not free-standing but attached to a wall.

ENTABLATURE the superstructure that is supported by columns consisting of architrave (resting directly on the columns), frieze (above the architrave) and projecting cornice, including gutter (at the top).

ETRUSCANS a people who lived to the north and south of Rome, who spoke a non-Indo-European language and who had an important political, religious and cultural influence on the early Romans.

Glossary

FAUCES entrance passage in a traditional Roman house leading to the atrium (9.1a).

FLUTES vertical channels carved in the shafts of columns: Doric columns usually have twenty flutes that meet in sharp arrises; Ionic usually have twenty-four, each separated from its neighbour by a fillet (flattened arris) (2.6 and 2.7).

FORESHORTENING the apparent shortening of the form of objects in relation to the angle from which they are observed; perspective applied to single objects or forms. For example, a horse seen from the rear will appear foreshortened (5.1).

FRIEZE the horizontal band of stones resting on top of the architrave. Doric friezes are divided into triglyphs and metopes. Ionic friezes are continuous.

GENRE PAINTING representations of everyday life (as opposed to mythological or historical pictures).

HELLENIC adjective used to describe Greek civilization from the time of the fall of the Mycenaeans until the time of Alexander the Great (356–323 BC) (derived from *Hellene*, the name by which the Greeks called themselves).

HELLENISTIC modern adjective used to describe the civilization in Greece and the lands conquered by Alexander the Great during the period 323–31 BC. Hellenistic tradition remained strong in the eastern part of the Roman empire even when political independence had been lost.

HIGH CLASSICAL period from about the middle to the end of the fifth century BC during which Pheidias and Polykleitos were active and the Parthenon was built.

HYDRIA water jar with three handles, two horizontal ones at the sides and a vertical one at the back for pouring (3.4).

IMPLUVIUM shallow pool in the atrium of a Roman house to catch the rainwater.

IONIANS people speaking the Ionian dialect of Greek and living chiefly on the islands of the Aegean, on the west coast of Asia Minor and in Athens.

IONIC ORDER an architectural system controlling the design of column and entablature (2.5).

KOUROS (plural: kouroi) archaic statue of a nude young man standing with one foot advanced and the weight evenly distributed between the two legs; made from the late seventh until the beginning of the fifth century BC (1.1, 1.6 and 1.9).

KRATER wide-mouthed bowl used for mixing wine and water (3.4).

KYLIX drinking cup (3.4).

LEKYTHOS narrow-necked container used for oil (3.4).

LOUTROPHOROS vessel used to carry the water for the ritual bath of brides; the shape was sometimes used for funerary monuments on the graves of unwed persons (3.4).

METOPES stone or terracotta panels inserted between pairs of triglyphs in a Doric frieze.

MODELLING (in painting) the technique of rendering the illusion of volume on a two-dimensional surface by means of shading.

MOSAIC technique of making a picture or design out of small pieces of stone of different colours. Stones are usually cut to be four-sided (for tesselated mosaics); glass is used only sparingly for floor mosaics, but much more abundantly for wall and ceiling mosaics.

MYCENAEAN the modern name given to the civilization of a people who spoke an early form of Greek and lived in Greece from the sixteenth to the twelfth centuries BC.

NAOS the central, inner part of a Greek temple, where the statue of the god was kept (literally: the dwelling of the god).

OINOCHOE jug (3.4).

OPISTHODOMOS porch at the back of the naos of a temple.

ORCHESTRA place of action for the chorus (and also the actors, until the Hellenistic period) in a Greek theatre (literally: dancing place).

ORTHOGONALS the receding lines that in a painting using single-point perspective converge at a single point.

PANHELLENIC 'all Greek' – a term used of festivals or sanctuaries that were common to all Greeks irrespective of whether they were Dorian or Ionian and of the polis they came from.

PEDIMENT triangular end of a gabled roof which could be filled with sculpture either carved in relief or free standing.

PERISTYLE a continuous colonnade surrounding either a building or a space; thus an external peristyle is the colonnade that surrounds a Greek temple (2.2) and an internal peristyle is the colonnade enclosing the space inside a courtyard, as in many Hellenistic and later Roman houses (6.1c and 9.1b).

PERSPECTIVE a technique for painting three-dimensional scenes on a two-dimensional surface to give the illusion of objects existing in space.

PILASTER   a shallow rectangular feature projecting from a wall having a capital and base, rather like an engaged half-column, but rectangular in section.

PODIUM   platform. The podium on which Roman temples were built was accessible by steps only from the front.

POLIS   (plural: poleis) independent communities usually comprising an urban centre together with the surrounding countryside; the political unit favoured by the Greeks during the archaic and classical periods.

POST-AND-LINTEL   structural system by which vertical posts (columns or walls) support horizontal lintels (architraves or ceilings).

PRONAOS   porch in front of the naos of a temple.

PROSKENION   colonnade between the orchestra and the scene building of a Greek theatre.

RED-FIGURE   technique of vase painting in which the figures are left in the natural colour of the vase and the background and details are painted black. The technique appears to have been invented in Athens around 530 BC and was very popular during the fifth and fourth centuries BC; it was used, often with the addition of much white and gold, in Sicily and south Italy during the fourth century BC.

RELIEF   sculpture which remains attached to the background, either very deeply carved (high relief) or shallowly carved (low relief).

SARCOPHAGUS   (plural: sarcophagi) carved marble coffin.

SCAENAE FRONS   (plural: scaenae frontes) the façade of the stage-building of a Roman theatre that formed the backdrop for the stage and was as high as the top seats of the auditorium.

SHAFT   main body of a column, between the base (if there is one) and the capital.

SIGNATURES (on vases)   signatures appear sporadically on Greek vases: those accompanied by the word 'egraphsen' (drew it) are presumably those of the painters; those accompanied by the word 'epoiesen' (made it) are presumably those of the potters. Some artists sign both egraphsen and epoiesen and therefore probably both made and painted the vase in question.

SKYPHOS   mug used for drinking (3.4).

STELE   (plural: stelai) an upright stone slab bearing a design or an inscription serving as a monument or marker.

STOA   a building with its roof partially supported by one or more rows of columns parallel to a rear wall.

STYLOBATE   top step of a temple, the platform on which the columns rest.

TABLINUM   central room at the far end of the atrium in a traditional Roman house (9.1a).

TORSO   what is left of the human body when the head and limbs have been removed.

TREASURY   a small building usually erected in a panhellenic sanctuary by a polis as a repository for its offerings to the god of the sanctuary.

TRIGLYPH   vertically grooved member of the Doric frieze.

VASE   conventional term used for Greek vessels made of pottery.

VAULT   arched roof.

VOLUTES   spiral scrolls curving to right and left decorating the front and back of Ionic capitals (2.5).

VOUSSOIR   wedge-shaped stone forming one of the units of an arch.

WHITE-GROUND LEKYTHOS   lekythos covered with a white slip (a thin coating of primary clay with little or no admixture of iron) on which, after the middle of the fifth century BC, the decoration was drawn in fugitive colours (mauves, blues and greens) which were applied *after* firing and so did not have the durability of the more usual rather restricted range of ceramic colours. Such vessels, which were too delicate for everyday use, were used to hold olive oil offered to the dead (3.15).

Further reading

GREEK ART

B. Ashmole *Architect and Sculptor in Classical Greece* (Phaidon 1972) architecture and architectural sculpture in the fifth and fourth centuries BC

J. D. Beazley and B. Ashmole *Greek Sculpture and Painting* (CUP 1932) from the geometric through the Hellenistic periods

J. Boardman *Greek Art* (Thames and Hudson 1973) paperback, general introduction with a short text and numerous illustrations

R. M. Cook *Greek Painted Pottery* (Methuen 1972) detailed handbook

W. B. Dinsmoor *The Architecture of Ancient Greece* (Batsford 1975) detailed standard reference work

R. Martin *Living Architecture: Greek* (Oldbourne 1967) illuminating brief introduction

J. J. Pollitt *Art and Experience in Classical Greece* (CUP 1972) paperback; sculpture, painting and architecture primarily in the fifth century BC

G. M. A. Richter *A Handbook of Greek Art* (Phaidon 1974) paperback, general introduction systematically covering many topics, including both major and minor arts

M. Robertson *A History of Greek Art* (CUP 1975) from the geometric through the Hellenistic periods excluding architecture; also available in a shortened version for less advanced students, *A Shorter History of Greek Art* (CUP 1981) paperback

S. Woodford *The Parthenon* (CUP 1981) paperback; sculpture, architecture, building procedures, early and later history

ROMAN ART

R. Bianchi Bandinelli *Rome, the Centre of Power* and *Rome, the Late Empire* (Thames and Hudson 1970 and 1971) general introduction copiously illustrated

A. Boethius and J. D. Ward-Perkins *Etruscan and Roman Architecture* (Pelican 1970) detailed standard work

G. M. A. Hanfmann *Roman Art* (Norton 1975) paperback, general introduction with a compendium of illustrations and commentary

H. Kähler *Rome and her Empire* (Methuen 1963) general introduction presenting the subject in chronological order

W. L. MacDonald *The Architecture of the Roman Empire* (Yale University Press 1965) detailed examination of important imperial works

P. MacKendrick *The Mute Stones Speak* (Norton 1976) paperback, general introduction to Roman art through the history of archaeological discoveries

G. M. A. Richter *Ancient Italy* (Michigan University Press 1955) wrong about the Etruscans, but valuable insights into Roman art

I. S. Ryberg *The Rites of the Roman State Religion in Art* (Memoirs of the American Academy in Rome, XXII, 1955) copiously illustrated intelligent analysis of numerous Roman reliefs

D. E. Strong *Roman Imperial Sculpture* (Tiranti 1961) introductory analysis of Roman reliefs

J. M. C. Toynbee *The Art of the Romans* (Thames and Hudson 1965) systematic handbook covering many topics, excluding architecture

LITERARY SOURCES

Pliny *The Elder Pliny's Chapters on the History of Art* (ed. Jex-Blake and Sellers) (Argonaut 1968) introduction, text in Latin and English carefully annotated

Pausanias *Guide to Greece* (Penguin 1971) 2 vols. paperback, English translation

J. J. Pollitt *The Art of Greece 1400–31 BC* and *The Art of Rome 753 BC–337 AD* (Prentice Hall, Sources and Documents, 1965 and 1966) paperback, translated selections from many different sources arranged in chronological blocks

Index